W9-CAY-968

CONSTRUCTING
TEDDY
AND HIS FRIENDS

BY JENNIFER LAING

Published by Hobby House Press, Inc.
Grantsville, Maryland
www.hobbyhouse.com

Hobby
House
Press

Dedication

This book is dedicated to the memory of a dear fellow bear artist, Shirley Kerr. She triumphed over adversity, and discovered in creating bears a whole new reason to live. Her life was an inspiration, and her love of bears was legendary.

All photography by Phillip Castleton of The Teddy Bear Shop, Sydney.
All styling by the author.

Cover and opposite page photo, showing all the patterns in the book:
Top row, L to R: Ickabod the four-legged Bear, ridden by Erik the Elf, Reggie the Rabbit and Bluegum the Koala.
Middle row, L to R: Ethel the Emu, ridden by Viola the Vervet Monkey, Nils the Gnome and Mortimer the Bear.
Front row, L to R: Phoebe the Panda, Philbert the Golly, Tom Collins the Pack Rat and Esme the Elephant.

Additional copies of this book may be purchased at $19.95 (plus postage and handling) from
Hobby House Press, Inc.
1 Corporate Drive, Grantsville, MD 21536
1-800-554-1447
www.hobbyhouse.com
or from your favorite bookstore or dealer.

©2002 by Jennifer Laing

All rights reserved. No part of this book may be reproduced or utilized in any form or by any means, electronic or mechanical, including photocopying, recording, or by an information storage and retrieval system, without permission in writing from the publisher. Inquiries should be addressed to Hobby House Press, Inc., 1 Corporate Drive, Grantsville, MD 21536.

Printed in the United States of America

ISBN: 0-87588-634-5

Contents

Introduction 6

Some Tips To Get You Started 8

England 14

Mortimer the Teddy Bear 15

Philbert the Golly 21

Europe 26

Erik the Elf 29

Nils the Gnome 35

America 39

Ickabod theFour-Legged Bear 40

Tom Collins the Pack Rat 51

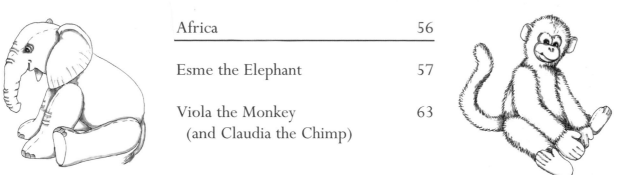

Africa   56

Esme the Elephant   57

Viola the Monkey   63
    (and Claudia the Chimp)

Asia   68

Phoebe the Panda   69

Australia   75

Bluegum the Koala   76

Ethel the Emu   83

Reggie the Rabbit   89

Conclusion   95
About the Author   96

Introduction

It has been well over a decade since I made my first teddy bear, and instantly became addicted to the art of making bears. They are still my passion, and my joy, and I would continue to create them even if I was the only person who liked them. The fact that they also bring joy to other people is such a bonus, and one I never take for granted. Over the years, however, I have occasionally designed and made a different little animal or two, to amuse and challenge myself. Sometimes these challenges have been thrown at me, as when my fellow Aussie artist Loris Hancock requested a frog in a bear swap. (She may be an excellent bear maker, but rather than collect bears, she is an ardent frog collector!) As I had never made a frog before I thought I should start at the beginning, so I made her a tadpole - with back legs. He was literally a work in progress.

Making a variety of animals is a wonderfully satisfying pastime, and can add to the skills we have already learned in making teddy bears. We can give them open mouths and realistic tongues, whiskers and tufted eyebrows, waxed noses, extra joints for increased pose-ability, wired ears, toes and tails. We can paint and shade their features in a variety of mediums. We can use up our scraps of fabrics, mohair and Ultrasuede, and go to town with needle-sculptured faces, hands and paws. The little critters we create could lead you off in a whole new direction (hmm…what about a line of sporting Gollies, feral gnomes or circus monkeys?), or just be a welcome friend for your bears.

The patterns are not made to any particular scale and most of them are fairly small. This is mainly because they are faster to make, take less mohair and fabric, and can easily be hand-sewn. Most of these patterns should be able to be made using scraps of fabrics you already have on hand, and all take less than a quarter yard (or meter) of mohair. If you prefer working to a larger scale, and like machine sewing, you can always enlarge the patterns on a photocopier. Just be aware that the three head pattern pieces (which in effect are three-dimensional) enlarge at a greater rate than the simpler two-piece (and two-dimensional) body and limb pieces. For this reason, try enlarging the head at a slightly smaller percentage than the rest of the pieces, then refer back to the original size pattern to check the head-to-body ratio. The patterns can also be reduced if you prefer.

In this book there are a dozen animal patterns for you to play with. They can all be made in a range of different fabrics and styles. Some of them even show you more than one variation on the pattern, for example Viola the Vervet Monkey can turn into Claudia the Chimp with a change of colors, different ears and without a tail. The baby elephant could become an adult with the addition of tusks, and the emu could turn into an ostrich with a change of color and the addition of fluffy wings. I didn't want this to be the sort of pattern book that says Polly Parrot has to be made out of red mohair and orange felt, and is supposed to look like this picture. Rather, I wanted to say; "Here is the pattern, I have made it up using these techniques, and here are a few variations made by some friends of mine to give you some ideas of how you might want to make it up. Now go and have fun, and do it your way!"

The group photos show you how different people can interpret the same pattern. Some of the animals were made by keen hobbyists, some were made by professional bear makers, but all have made a valuable contribution to show the diversity that individual expression and imagination produces. The point is not to try and make the pattern 'look like the picture', but instead to put your twist on it, and to create something that comes from you.

Each animal has some feature that makes it a bit more advanced than your standard pattern. Don't be put off if you are inexperienced, however, just leave out the bits that you don't like. The rat will work equally well without a wired tail, or you could pour the tiniest glass pellets into his tail to weight it instead. The teddy bear will be fine without any details to his paws if sculpting the toes does not work for you.

If you fancy more of a challenge, you can always make the patterns more elaborate. The four-legged bear, for example, looks great with an inset Ultrasuede muzzle, which is then needle-sculpted to create wrinkles, lips, eyelids etc.. You can always add a couple of white beads stitched to the lower mouth edge to give him teeth. Add shading to the muzzle along with the needle-sculpture and you have a character that looks really alive. The panda looks fantastic with appliquéd pawpads of Ultrasuede over a mohair base, so that the pad details realistically poke through the fur on the feet.

Don't be frightened of playing around with your mohair to achieve the look you want. Try over-dying, especially on the tipped mohairs like the Zotty and the Mecki (named after the Steiff® bear and hedgehog which use these Schulte mohair styles). Even a simple soaking in a strong coffee or tea solution can give you a subtle change of color and shade, and works well to soften a mohair color that has a light backing.

The stuffing can also play an important part in the way the animal looks, poses and feels.

Experiment with a combination of stuffing materials, and with stuffing at least parts of the animal softly. It is harder to stuff softly than it is to stuff firmly, but your finished animal will often pose in a floppier, more realistic way, and will certainly be nicer to cuddle up with.

Measurements are given in both imperial and metric, as both systems are often used simultaneously in the teddy bear world. It seems odd but is quite common to say, for example, that you are making a 10in (25cm) bear and need 6mm eyes for it, and that it will take a quarter of a meter of 3/8in (.9cm) pile mohair to make it!

To make the pattern ready to use, you can photocopy the pattern pages, and then glue the sheets to cardboard and then cut out the pattern pieces. Alternatively, you can place the paper patterns under a sheet of plastic template and draw them on, then cut them out. Simply place a sheet of clear template plastic (available from bear making suppliers and patchwork quilt making suppliers) directly over the printed pattern and trace around the pieces. Using a plastic template will be easier for you if you wish to modify the pattern to give your animal an inset muzzle or chest. This enables you to see where to add a seam allowance to the sections to be cut and inset. Cut out your cardboard or plastic pieces carefully with scissors (not your good ones!), and make sure to punch out the joint holes. Write on each piece any important informa-tion such as openings, fur direction etc. Keep your working pattern in a plastic zip-lock bag with a stick-on label to identify it. Your patterns can then be filed when not in use.

(Please note: as with all other commercial kits and patterns world-wide, the patterns in this book are copyright protected and therefore not for re-sale and the animals made from these patterns cannot be sold. They are for your enjoyment only.)

Some Tips To Get You Started

MARKING OUT

Always take a good look at your piece of mohair before starting to mark out. Frequently, you will find that the direction of the fur varies (Fig. 1), even with straight mohair. On a curly or distressed piece, the fur direction will be even harder to determine! If you find it really hard to determine the fur direction, looking at the back of the fabric will help. The nap or direction of the fur will be where the fur is seen over the edge of the piece of fabric. You will need to take the fur direction into account, as well as the actual weave of the fabric (the warp and the weft). The weave of the fabric is where it's strength lies, and as the warp and the weft run vertically and horizontally, that is the way the pattern pieces need to be placed, in order not to stretch and distort once they are stuffed. If the pieces are marked out on the diagonal, this is the stretchy part of the fabric, and you will find that this will lead to asymmetrical distortion when stuffed. This is something you definitely do not want!

When marking out your pattern pieces on mohair, look first in the corners of the fabric for suitable fur direction, and lay out your side head pattern pieces and gusset first. These are the most important pieces to get the fur direction right on, but they also need to be laid out in the strength of the grain, that is, either horizontally or vertically. (See Fig. 2.) The rest of the pattern pieces can then be laid out, but leave the ears, tails, and other small pieces until last. You will always find little spaces to squeeze them into, and you will make better use of your fabric that way.

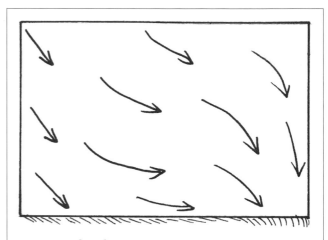

1. How fur direction can vary over your piece of mohair.

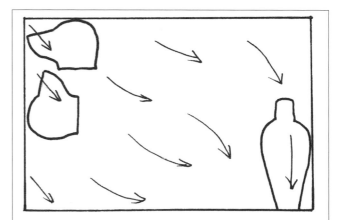

2. Laying out the head and gusset first, paying attention to both the fur direction and the grain of the fabric.

CUTTING AND PINNING

Cut out all the pieces carefully, using small, sharp pointed scissors to avoid chopping the fur off the edges. Pin the pieces together in their pairs to avoid confusing leg shapes, or losing little pieces like ears. It is a good idea to trim away the fur on your seam allowance (that is a maximum of ¼in [.65cm]) around the head pattern pieces. This will give you a professional, seamless appearance. On dense or tipped mohair, this trimming works well around each pattern piece before sewing. Make sure that you do not cut off more than the seam allowance, or you will end up with a bare "fire break" strip at the sewn seams.

Use your pins to tuck any stray hair inside the pieces, leaving you a clean edge to sew. After sewing, turn your pieces right-side out and brush out the seams to pull out any trapped fur. If you use your pins with the points facing into the middle of the pieces you are working on, and with the points tucked inside, it helps prevent the pieces from puckering. It also stops your thread from catching on the points when hand-sewing.

SEWING

The patterns can be either hand-sewn or machine-sewn. If hand-sewing, remember that a firm tension is important, possibly more so than stitch size. You can use either a backstitch or a reverse running-stitch if you are hand-sewing, and often a quick overcasting stitch first helps to hold together any tricky pieces or thick fur. If machine-sewing, you might still like to hand-baste or tack your pieces together first. This means you can remove the pins before machine stitching, and also prevents any fur from poking through the seams.

Your seam allowance will vary according to the size of the animal you are making, but try never to work too close to the edge, or you will find that the fabric will fray and pull apart when it is stuffed. The minimum seam allowance for mohair is around ⅛in (.31cm) or 3mm on a small bear, but you can work closer to the edge when using Ultrasuede. All these patterns are designed for a perfect fit, so they should go together easily for you. The necks on the body pieces are to be sewn right across, leaving only a small spot open centrally for the neck joint. They do not need to be left open across the neck and then gathered. Any darts are to be sewn closed first, before sewing the matching pieces together. As an aside, it doesn't really matter whether you cut out the darts or merely mark them without cutting into the V-shape of the dart. The only difference will be, if you have cut out the dart, your seam line - and your dart, will be a little wider when you sew the dart up than if you only marked it and sewed it on the line.

When sewing in footpads, the pinning is all-important for an even fit. First find the center of the toe on the pad, pin that into the central toe seam, then repeat with the heel. After these two pins, then place a pin in the middle of each side, attaching the pad to the mohair edge. These four pins should hold the footpad in squarely, but you might want to place in another four pins in the gaps of a larger footpad to ensure a smooth fit when sewing.

There are several ways to sew a gusset into the head pieces, but this is possibly the easiest way, and one that ensures a perfect fit. It is vital to get the gusset sewn in evenly; otherwise the head will distort when stuffing. First sew the two side head pieces together, from the tip of the nose to the bottom of the neck (Fig. 3). Next, pin in the muzzle of the gusset, using the center of the nose and the "eye spots" (that angle where the straight line of the muzzle finishes, and the curve of the forehead starts) as your reference points. (Fig.4) Add more pins to the outer corners of the muzzle edge, and to the sides of the muzzle, as in Fig 5. The seam from one "eye spot" to the other can now be sewn around the U-shape on the top of the muzzle.

Next, pin the back corner of the neck on the gusset to the matching edge of the head side piece, and ease in around the curve of the head with your pinning. This will ensure that the edges match up perfectly, something that will not happen if you pin back from your sewn muzzle to the neck edges. The rest of the head can then be sewn.

While this is the regular way of sewing the head pieces together, there are always alternatives, particularly when the pattern is quite difficult to work with. The Tom Collins Pack Rat pattern is one example of a different way of assembling the head.

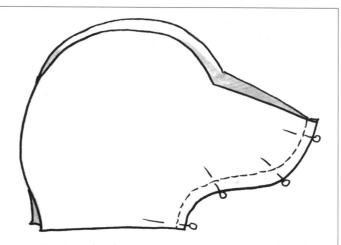

3. Sewing the first seam on the two side head pieces.

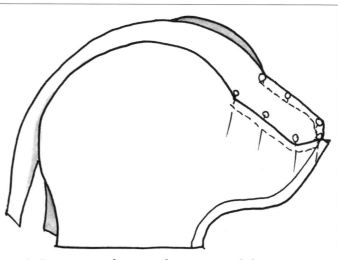

4. Pinning in the muzzle section of the gusset.

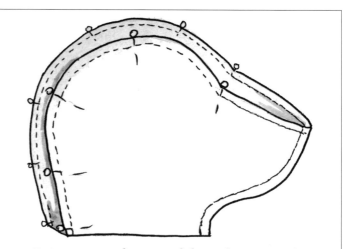

5. Pinning in the rest of the tail section of the gusset.

An important note on the pawpads in some of these patterns:

The pawpads on the arms of the bear, panda and koala patterns have been designed for extra curvature of the arm. That means that no allowance has been given for the wrist seam, which, when the pawpad is sewn into the inner arm makes the inner arm slightly shorter than the outer arm. Don't panic, this is meant to be! It will work in your favor, provided you pin it correctly. To pin the inner arm to the outer arm, start pinning at the top of the shoulder and work down to the wrist. Now you are left with the difference all in the pawpad area, and you have ensured that the arm opening has equal sides which will give you a smooth closing seam.

With the difference now apparent in the pad area, you will see that the pawpad is shorter than the back of the paw. Put your first pin in the center tip of the paw, which halves the problem. You should now be able to ease in the extra fabric around either half of the pawpad with your pins, without having any puckers. What you will notice is that this pinning of a short side to a slightly longer side creates a curving effect, and pulls the wrist in towards the body slightly. This curving of the paws gives a nice, natural effect, and the curvature can be increased further by sculpting fingers or toes (See page 42 for details).

Before turning your sewn pieces through, you can protect the edges of the openings with Fray-Check type glue if they look like they might fray or wear. Watered-down PVA or craft glue (50% glue mixed with 50% water in a nozzle squeeze-bottle) is perfect and really cheap.

Ladder-stitch is the perfect stitch for closing your seams after stuffing, as it gives you a smooth, invisible seam even though it is stitched from the outside. Use a strong thread for closing your seams, such as upholstery thread (the Mastex brand is a popular one), and pull tight after every couple of stitches. Start at the top of the opening and stitch down, as this will also follow the fur direction and be easier than working against the flow of the fur. Begin your ladder-stitch from the inside of the opening, and a little above it, next to the seam. (See #1 on Fig.6) Make sure that your stitches are even, both in the distance apart and in the depth back from the fabric edge (keep your normal seam allowance as a guideline for that.) Even stitches, as in Fig. 6, will create the parallel rungs of your ladder, and will also prevent the seam from puckering. Finish off by knotting over an old thread in the seam and sink the knot by pulling the thread inside the stuffing, bringing it out away from the knot and cutting it off close to the fabric.

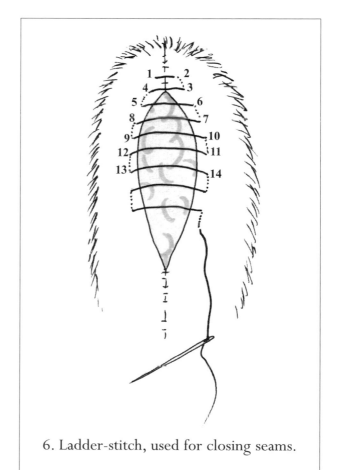

6. Ladder-stitch, used for closing seams.

JOINTS

There are a variety of jointing systems available for making bears and other animals. Many professionals use more than one system, depending on the size of the animal they are making.

Cotter pins are great for smaller animals (up to, 6in [15cm] in size) but are often not strong or durable enough for the larger ones. Cotter pin keys are used to turn the ends of the pin down, rather like opening a tin of anchovies with the little key it comes with. When using a cotter pin joint, the limb can be stuffed and closed before attaching it to the body, as a single tool on the inside of the body is all that is needed for fastening.

Locknuts and bolts provide strength, non-slip durability and a little extra weight for larger bears and animals. The limb needs to be attached to the body before it is stuffed or closed, as it has to be accessible from both sides of the joint. Two tools are needed, one to hold the head of the bolt still inside the limb, and one to tighten down the nut inside the body cavity. The nylon ring inside the locknut holds the nut in place once it has been tightened to your satisfaction. The tools that you use with locknuts and bolts can be ring spanners, wrenches, nut drivers or even ratchet spanners. Choose the perfect size tool for your locknuts. I usually use a $^5/_{16}$in (.75cm) nut for small animals 6in (15cm) to 10in (25cm) and a $^7/_{16}$in (1cm) nut for anything over 10in (25cm.) in size. This might seem quite large and heavy, but I like the extra bit of weight the hardware in the joints gives the animals, and it means that you don't have to

add pellets or steel shot to increase the weight as you do with small cotter pin jointed animals.

The neck joint is one which needs to be fastened from the inside of the body, once the head has been closed. (You can try leaving a hole in the back gusset of the head, in order to hold the head of the bolt still with a tool. This often leads to an unsatisfactory head shape, however, with dips and soft spots.) This means that a standard locknut cannot be successfully used. (It can be forced on while holding the shaft of the bolt still with a pair of vice-grips, but this technique can occasionally strip the thread on the bolt and make fastening the nut impossible. Alternatively, if you glue the washer and disc to the head of the bolt, and stuff the head really firmly, you can often get a locknut on the neck joint without the bolt moving. This technique is also not 100 percent reliable, and can lead to frustration!)

Many professionals use a cotter pin for the neck joint, and locknuts and bolts for the limbs. Another alternative is to use a grub screw, sometimes called an "Arizona bolt" for the neck. This particular kind of screw has a hexagonal hole in the end, which fits an Allen key. This enables you to place a ring spanner on the locknut and to fasten it down from one side only, while holding the shaft of the bolt still with the Allen key. Yet another alternative is to fasten on an ordinary nut onto the bolt of your neck joint, tighten it down with your spanner or wrench, then turn it into a locknut by adding a drop of Superglue or Loktite around the thread on the inside edge of the nut.

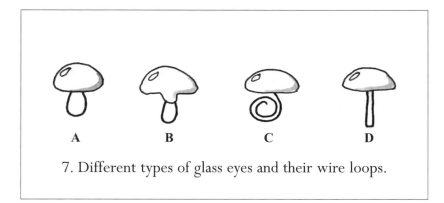

7. Different types of glass eyes and their wire loops.

EYES

For all the patterns in this book, glass eyes on wire loops are recommended. If you have antique boot buttons in the size you want they are wonderful, but often are only available in a limited range of sizes (usually 7 to 10mm). You can get different quality glass eyes, as well as plain black or in a wide variety of colors with pupils. Also available are different wire backs, as illustrated in Fig. 7.

The narrow wire shown in Fig. 7D is useful in that is does not need to be pinched closed before pulling the eye into the head. With the eye wire on Fig. 7A you will need to use pliers to pinch it closed after you have threaded it onto your needle, but before you pull it into the thread. With the styles of wire in Fig. 7B and C, you will not be able to easily pinch the loop closed, and you will need to use an awl to punch a hole in the "eye spot" in order to sink the eye properly into the head. The same is true when using antique boot buttons, as they have a heavy shank.

England

This is where the teddy bear really took hold as the first, and often the most enduring, love of our lives. England is the land of famous bear characters, like Winnie-the-Pooh, Paddington, Rupert and Sooty. Even though the teddy bear began in Germany, (with America quick on its heels), many people tend to think of England as the spiritual birthplace of the teddy. It is therefore fitting to include a classic bear, with an old English name, to celebrate the centenary of the teddy bear in 2002.

Mortimer
the Teddy Bear

Mortimer the Bear, made in straight mohair with
Ultrasuede sculpted or 'pulled' toes.

Mortimer
An 8in (20cm) Bear

Mortimer the bear is simple to make, with a quick two-piece body. In spite of this simple body shape, there are darts at the neck and at the bottom of the body pieces, which add shaping to the shoulders and base of the body. Darts are always sewn closed first before sewing around the rest of the piece.

He looks great in a variety of mohair styles, straight, or distressed, dense to sparse. Play around with him and see what you like the best. Because he is a small bear he is quick to hand-sew, and he is easy to make. Note the explanation on sewing the arms on page 11 before construction.

Stitching the Nose

His nose is the simplest, most foolproof style, using the gusset seams for a guideline (See Fig. 8). Use a double thread of your DMC #5, and place the point of the needle between the two threads each time you start a stitch. By doing this you will ensure that the stitch lies flat and does not twist. (Do not bring your needle out between the threads of your last stitch, or this will create a twisted chain stitch at the end of each stitch). A simple fly-stitch A-B, C-D creates an edge for the nose and an anchoring point for the mouth. Feed your needle behind your C-D stitch to create a single stitch E-F. A long stitch for the mouth will give you a better smile than a short stitch.

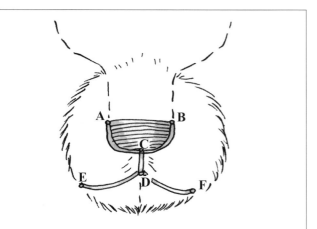

8. Stitching a simple horizontal nose.

Needle-Sculpture For the Eyes

There is quick and easy needle-sculpture in his eye socket area, prior to placing in the eyes (See Fig. 9). Needle-sculpture is simply taking a good, strong thread such as an upholstery thread on a doll- making needle, and stitching in areas which need to be pulled, tightened or lifted. By stitching several times from "eye spot" to "eye spot", in the gusset seam and through the muzzle at A-B, and then pulling, you can create deepened eye sockets and also narrow the bridge of the nose. After needle sculpting has been done, and eye sockets have been created, the eyes can then be sewn in.

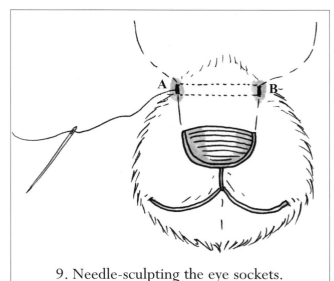

9. Needle-sculpting the eye sockets.

Sewing In the Eyes

This is the simplest way of placing in the eyes. Thread each eye on a strong thread (artificial sinew is great for this), and place the ends of the threads into the eye of a doll-making needle long enough to reach through the head. The eyes are positioned close to the gusset seams, below the angle of gusset as it widens into the forehead, and to the outside of the seam. The needle is simply positioned where you want the eye, and then the needle is brought out at the base of the neck, as close to the disc as possible. The second eye's thread is brought out close to the first, and the two threads are tightly knotted together. The knot is then sunk by putting both threads onto the needle, sinking them by stitching down next to the knot, bringing the threads out away from the knot, pulling and cutting them off short.

Joints

His joints are the simplest type, T-headed cotter pins, sometimes known as T-pins. These are good for a small bear or animal, but may not be strong enough for a large one. See the introduction on joints on page 12 for further details.

Ears

Mortimer's ears have the raw edges turned inside the ear and are sewn closed, then placed halfway through the depth of the head when viewed from the top. Use the gusset seam as a guideline and pin in the top edge. Curve the ear around your thumb and pin in the bottom edge in a curved "C" shape. Use a third pin to secure the center of the curve of the ear. The ear should now have a nicely curved shape, with the top of the ear being slightly further forward than the bottom of the ear. This will give it a realistic look. Make sure to pin both ears on before sewing, in order to get them even. The ears can be either ladder-stitched around the back curve of the ear, or sewn on with a zigzag stitch from each side. This latter method has to be done by feel rather than by sight, especially when working from the inside of the curve.

Feet Details

His big feet can be given extra detail if you wish. See Ickabod the American four-legged bear for pawpad options, including sculpted or pulled toes.

When you are stuffing the body, you can add some pellets or beads if you want to give your bear a soft, squishy feel. The pellets will also help to weight the bear, which he will need, as the cotter pin joints are very light. Place stuffing in the top and bottom of the body cavity first, making sure that you have covered the joints. A small amount of pellets can then be poured into the center of the body, along with some small soft pieces of stuffing. This stuffing will help keep the pellets suspended and prevent them from clumping. Under-stuff rather than over-stuff to keep the body soft when the seam is closed.

Materials Required:

Fur- 1/8 yd (or meter) of mohair with a 3/8in (.9cm) pile.

Paws- 3½in (9cm) x 4½in (12cm) x 11½cm of Ultrasuede for paws.

Joints- 10-1in (25mm) discs with a small hole. 5-small T-headed cotter pins.

Eyes- one pair of 5mm black glass.

Nose and claws- DMC #5.

Polyfill stuffing, plus some glass beads for the tummy.

A mob of Mortimers in different types of mohair, made by: Back row, L to R: Lesley Neuhaus, Susan Carroll, Kathy Sewell and Julie Blake. Front row, L to R: Louise Humphries, Leanne Triggs, the author, and Vicki-Lynn Smith.

Mortimer Patterns

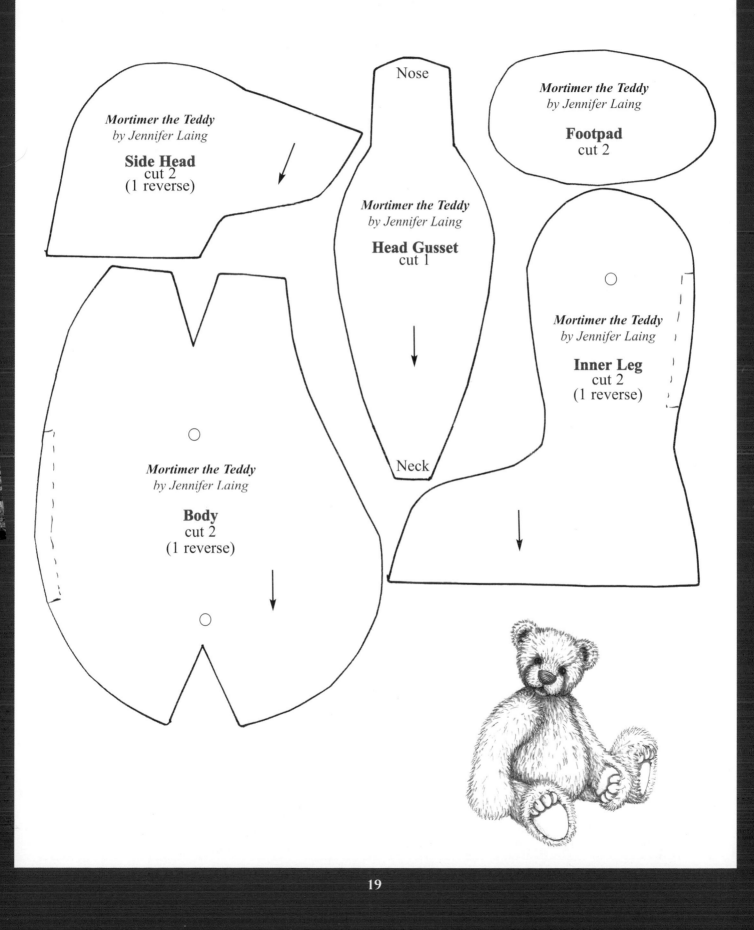

Mortimer the Teddy
by Jennifer Laing

Side Head
cut 2
(1 reverse)

Nose

Mortimer the Teddy
by Jennifer Laing

Footpad
cut 2

Mortimer the Teddy
by Jennifer Laing

Head Gusset
cut 1

Mortimer the Teddy
by Jennifer Laing

Inner Leg
cut 2
(1 reverse)

Neck

Mortimer the Teddy
by Jennifer Laing

Body
cut 2
(1 reverse)

Mortimer Patterns

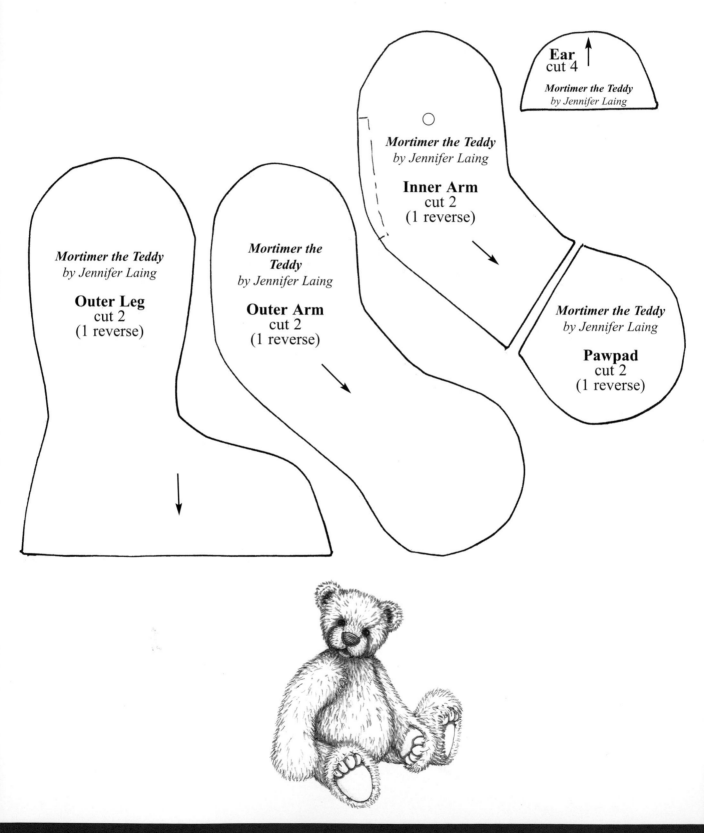

Ear
cut 4

Mortimer the Teddy
by Jennifer Laing

Mortimer the Teddy
by Jennifer Laing

Inner Arm
cut 2
(1 reverse)

Mortimer the Teddy
by Jennifer Laing

Pawpad
cut 2
(1 reverse)

Mortimer the Teddy
by Jennifer Laing

Outer Leg
cut 2
(1 reverse)

Mortimer the Teddy
by Jennifer Laing

Outer Arm
cut 2
(1 reverse)

Philbert the Golly

Philbert
A 5in (13cm) Golly

Golliwogs were thought to have originated in America in the early 1900s, a result of illustrator Florence Upton's imagination, but as with the teddy, they quickly became embraced by English adults and children alike. Often homemade out of felt, fabrics, or even knitted, they were also commercially produced (Steiff® made them from 1913 onwards, as well as Chad Valley, Merrythought and Dean's) and became the symbol of the ever-popular Robertson's marmalade. Gollies are enjoying a well-deserved resurgence in popularity today. Gollies had almost always been male, but recently girl Gollies and baby Gollies have started to join them. Traditionally, the Golly was dressed in a frock coat and bow tie, but lately we have started seeing sporting Gollies, clown Gollies and other quite casual Gollies. Gollies are definitely taking on a life of their own.

Philbert is a little Golly, designed to be a companion to the small bear Montgomery, but he could easily be made smaller or larger if you wish. This tiny Golly can be made out of scraps of Ultrasuede, miniature velvet and thin fabrics. His hair can be hand-tufted using a DMC #8 thread, creating the look of dreadlocks. If you prefer, you could glue on some short pile mohair instead, following the dotted line on the head pattern piece, and attaching it after the head has been stuffed. He can also be made as a "she" and you can create a Philomena wearing a ribbon skirt and some flowers and bows.

The Head

Sew the darts closed on the head pieces before sewing the head together. Sew each hand to the arm at the wrist before sewing the arm pieces together. When sewing is complete place the joints in the limbs, stuff and sew closed with ladder-stitch. If you want him to stand you can fill the feet, up to the ankles, with the finest glass beads. This will give him some weight, and better balance. The hands can be stitched through to create fingers, as detailed in the pattern.

Stuff the head, and glue the mouth in place. Using a strong thread, before placing in the eyes, stitch between the eyes A-B and pull to form deepened sockets. Continue with the thread and stitch from the eye sockets down to each corner of the mouth and pull upward to the same eye socket A-a, then B-b as in Fig.10. A final stitch from the eye sockets A-B and through the middle of the mouth at C will create shaped lips. The eyes are then ready to be sewn in.

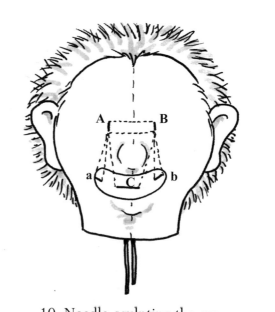

10. Needle-sculpting the eye sockets and mouth on the Golly.

Cut out some small white Ultrasuede circles using a hole punch, and thread one on behind the eye bead before placing in the eye. This will back the eye with a white ring; outlining it and making the eye stand out. If you experiment with this, you can make your Golly look to one side if you prefer, rather like a googly-eyed doll.

The ears should be sewn on before adding the hair, curving them in a natural shape with your pinning.

His hair can be either hand-tufted, using a double thread of DMC # 8 (See tufting description for the eyebrows of Nils the Gnome), or can be cut out of a scrap of black mohair and glued in place, using a tacky glue. Once the head is complete and jointed to the body, stuff and close the body and you are ready to add the finishing clothes.

The pants are designed to be quite tight, and they are difficult to get over his big feet if sewn up separately and then pulled on. If you are using a frail fabric, glue the edges with a protective Fray-Check type sealer and let dry before cutting the pieces out. Start from the bottom edge of the cuff, sew up the inside leg seam to the crotch, and then sew up the front seam to the waist band. Repeat on the other inside leg, sewing up the back seam to the waist. You will find it easier to actually pin the open-sided pants onto the body at this stage, then ladder-stitch the outside leg seams closed while on the Golly. If your Golly is a little slimmer (it all depends on your stuffing and on the stretchiness of the body fabric), you may need to trim a little off the pants' waistband area as you sew it up.

His frock coat has a glued-on collar, cuffs and also has a glued-on shirt collar, and dickey front, creating a shirt. For ease of assembly, this order works best. First glue on the dickey front, then the collar. Add the cuffs, and then the tails, pulling the tabs at the sides of the tails around at the front to form a waistband. Glue on the lapels, covering the edge of the dickey front, and the front join of the waistband. Finally, glue on the tab at the back of the tailcoat, covering the edge of the tails at the waist. You can then stitch on beads for buttons, at either side of the back tab, on the cuff and on the front of the coat jacket at the waist. Gold beads create nice gold buttons for the coat. Different colored beads can then be sewn on to create shirtfront buttons. You can also add a buttonhole bouquet, and tie a thin ribbon around his neck to give him a bow tie.

Girl Gollies

If your Philbert is to be a Philomena, make her legs in black, like her hands. Instead of "dressing" her in a frock coat and pants, you can make a skirt out of a 6in (12cm) length of wide ribbon. Simply gather one edge on a thread with a running-stitch, and tie it around her waist. The ends of the ribbon can be sewn together first if you wish to create a loop. If you are using a wired ribbon, simply pull the wire out of one edge, and ruche the ribbon by pulling on both ends of the other wire. This wire can then be twisted together to attach the skirt onto the body. Philomena can be decorated with flowers of ribbons in her hair, around her cuffs and neck, and buttons (seed beads) can be sewn down the front of her bodice.

Materials Required

Ultrasuede- black for head, ears and hands-
  4in x 4in (10cm x 10cm)
miniature velvet- for body and arms-
  5in x 4in (13cm x 10cm)
 miniature velvet- for legs and footpads-
  5in x 3½in (13cm x 9cm)
Fine fabric for pants-
  5in x 3in (13cm x 8cm)
Eyes- one pair of 3mm black onyx beads.
Hair- knotted black DMC# 8, or a scrap of
  black mohair.
Joints- 10 - ³⁄₈ in/10mm discs and
  5 - mini T-cotter pins.
Polyfill stuffing.
Ribbon and seed beads for accessorizing.

Philbert the Golly, standing on a very useful old book,
hand bound by Terry Collins.

Philbert Patterns

Philbert the Golly
by Jennifer Laing
Head
cut 2 (1 reverse)

Philbert the Golly
by Jennifer Laing
Hair
cut 2
(1 reverse)

Ear
cut 2
(1 reversed)
PTG

Philbert the Golly by Jennifer Laing
Cuffs - cut 2

Philbert the Golly by Jennifer Laing
Collar - cut 1

Coat Detail
cut 1 *PTG*

Philbert the Golly
by Jennifer Laing
Tails
cut 1

Mouth
PTG

Philbert the Golly
by Jennifer Laing
Arm
cut 4 (2 reverse)

Philbert the Golly
by Jennifer Laing
Hand
cut 4 (2 reverse)

Philbert the Golly
by Jennifer Laing

Philbert the Golly
by Jennifer Laing
Body
cut 2 (1 reverse)

Philbert the Golly
by
Jennifer Laing
Leg
cut 4 (2 reverse)

Philbert the Golly
by Jennifer Laing
Pants
cut 2

Philbert the Golly
by Jennifer Laing
Lapels - cut 1

Philbert the Golly
by Jennifer Laing
Dickey Front
cut 1

Philbert the Golly
by Jennifer Laing
Foot - cut 4 (2 reverse)

✿ Black
✳ Coat Color
◻ Brown
✾ White
(Mouth in pink)

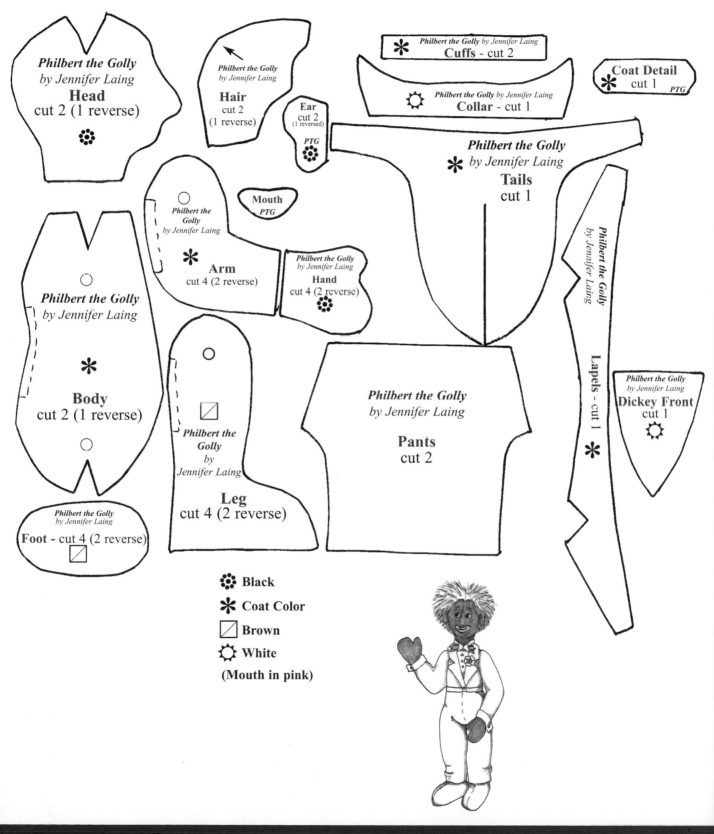

Europe

Europe is the place for fairy tales, the lands of gnomes, goblins, sprites, elves, trolls, pixies and all manner of dragonish, mystical beasts. Even Santa Claus started off as a gnome in Europe. In Sweden, Tomten is the character who visits homes on Christmas Eve with a toy-filled sack, and who eats the rice pudding and ginger biscuits left out for him. He is a shy but sweet forest gnome who also takes care of the animals during the long, cold winters. Elves are traditionally tall and thin, and can either be dark or blonde, but are usually young, sometimes even immortal!

Steiff® designed many fantastic felt dolls from 1892 till around 1930, and these have been the inspiration for the elf and gnome patterns in this book. Steiff®'s dolls often had wit and humor, and all had great character. The early Steiff® felt dolls also demonstrated their superlative construction by often having hand-tufted hair rather than glued on wigs. The Snik and Snak gnomes which Steiff® made from 1911 till the 1930s are a wonderful example of this, having hand-tufted eyebrows and beards. Their pointed caps hid their sweet bald heads, and they even had slip-on wooden and leather clogs on their large feet.

These gnome and elf patterns are very economical to make, and use up scraps of mohair, felt, Ultrasuede and mini. upholstery velvet. They also make great accessories for bears, as well as adapting to become Santa's helpers at Christmas time. If you are using felt, always make sure it is the pure wool felt rather than the cheap acrylic craft felt, as it is much stronger and nicer to use. Rather than making up the patterns all in felt or all in Ultrasuede, they have more texture and work better when a variety of Ultrasuede, felt and mini. velvets are used. If you want to paint fine details such as eyebrows on the face, however, it is better to use Ultrasuede for the flesh rather than felt, as there will be less smudging.

When sewing, sew the front and back of the head together before sewing the two halves together around the profile. Sew the ear pieces together, and when turned through, stitch around the rim as illustrated in the pattern. Alternatively, you could make the ear out of a single layer of your fabric, and just paint on some shading. Sew the hand onto each arm piece before sewing your arms together, and sew the boot sole into the bottom of the sewn leg just like putting in a bear's footpad. (The boot sole on the elf pattern only reaches the flat base of the boot, not the pointed toe.) The hands can be stitched through to create fingers, as shown in the pattern.

Stuff the head and joint it at the neck, closing it securely with a gathering and darning stitch. Before placing in the eyes, needle-sculpt the eye sockets by stitching between the eyes with a strong thread and pulling together. Dimples can be created for the edges of the mouth by stitching down from each eye socket area to make a small stitch at the corner of the mouth, and then pulling back up to the eye area. Knot it off at the base of the neck to anchor it securely. Sew in the eyes, knotting them firmly down at the edge of the neck, as close to the neck disc as possible. Then sew on the ears, which are pinned in a natural, curved position approximately level with the eye sockets.

Hand-Tufting

Hand-tufting is a great way of adding character to your creation. It is a simple technique, and can be used with a variety of fibers. For example: horsehair to create whiskers as we do for our Pack Rat Tom Collins, DMC thread to create dreadlocks or cornrows for our Gollies, or mohair hanks to create eyebrows, moustaches, beards or even a comb-over hairstyle on our gnome. It can also be used to introduce a second color in a face on a bear, particularly when you just want a hint of color, or when using black or very dark fur. Think of the tan eyebrow dots found on black dogs like Dobermans, these are also often found on black bears! Perhaps you might want to give your bear a moustache, to make him an old man bear, or give your bear long hair to make it into a girl bear like Rapunzel. The mohair hanks or mohair rovings are long strands of natural mohair, which have been cleaned and dyed, ready for craft use. You can always dye natural hanks if there is a particular color you are trying to match. If you can't find horsehair or mohair hanks in your local craft stores, try Tandy Craft Supplies in the United States for horsehair and specialty knitting and yarn stores for raw mohair. You may even know someone who has horse or breeds angora goats and get it from the source!

Hand-tufting is a technique that can also re-thatch a balding teddy, if you can match the color well and have patience. It would be recommended for covering a bald spot rather than replacing an entire fur coat, unless you have plenty of time on your hands. An interesting aside here is that in the early 1980s, talented artist Regina Brock from Ohio wanted to make bears but couldn't find mohair fabric, so created completely hand-tufted mohair bears working from a linen form as a 'skin'. Because of the time involved, Regina did not make many bears each year, but each of her bears was exquisitely made. She now specializes in beautiful, large, antique Steiff®-like bears (made of traditional mohair fabric) but still uses her unique tufting techniques to restore balding antique bears.

For tufting you will need your horsehair for whiskers or mohair for hair or fur, and a 3in (8cm) doll-making needle. Place a small strand through the needle at a time, trimming the ends of your strand straight first to make it easier to thread. If using mohair you can wet and twist the end of the strand to help threading also. The idea of tufting is to leave a securely anchored tuft of hair in the place that you want it, with both ends of the strand acting as part of the tuft. In order to achieve this, keep the slashing "Z" for Zorro in mind, see Fig. 11. Just as you would write the letter Z, put your needle in at the start, and come out at the end of the horizontal stroke. Pull your hair through until it is roughly the length you want. You may need to anchor down the start of the tuft with a finger to stop it from slipping through at this stage. Put your needle back in, making a small stitch, and create

the diagonal stroke, coming back out close to where your tuft started, but not at the same spot. Finally, put your needle back in, making your last horizontal stroke, and bring it out where you want the other end of the tuft. This Z-stroke stitch anchors each end of your tuft, making it impossible to pull out. Your "Z" can be narrow, and produce one double-ended tuft, or your could make it a wide one and produce two single ended tufts, as in working across the eyebrows at once.

For tufted mohair eyebrows, match your mohair color to your hair and skin-tones. Each eyebrow can be made up of three or more tufts, depending how bushy you want them and how thick your strands are. The hair can be trimmed to the length you want and shaped by wetting and combing it, or even using clear hair gel, then brushing out the stiffness when dry.

Similarly, whiskers look good in groups of three, with approximately three horsehair strands in each needle load. When using horsehair, you can curve it by using your thumbnail, pinching each hair and running your nail along the underside, just as you do with scissors when curling package ribbon. Whiskers look natural when trimmed to varying lengths, and not too long.

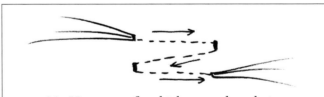

11. How to tuft whiskers and mohair.

Erik the Elf

Erik
A 10in (25cm) Elf

Erik is a tall, gangly young elf, who can be made in a variety of styles and colors. He looks great as a blond Scandinavian character, or in the browns and greens of a woodland sprite. Accessories such as acorns, mushrooms and birds' nests suit a woodland elf, or he could be in the reds and greens of a Santa's helper.

The Head

Sew the mohair to each face side piece, before sewing the halves together. Turn and stuff the head, and then needle-sculpt it between the eyes A-B and the corners of the mouth. Pull the corners of the mouth up to the eye sockets to lift the mouth into a smile, from a-A and b-B, as in Fig.12. Bring the needle out at the neck opening, and use it to gather around the opening, first placing in the joint and then closing tightly around it. The eyes can then be sewn in, pulling them in firmly and knotting off at the lowest possible point of the neck, next to the neck joint.

Features can be added with indelible art marker pens, or even with watercolor pencils or powder eye shadow and blush. Eyebrows can be either drawn on or tufted with mohair rovings that match the color of the mohair hair. If your young elf is fair or a redhead, he might look good with freckles!

The Ears

The ears can be made up either with a single thickness of flesh-tone Ultrasuede, or two sewn layers. If using two layers, sew them together, turn them through, and then stitch a line around the edge to form the rim of the ear and to give it definition. The pattern piece gives you an idea of how you can stitch this area. Turn the edges of the opening under and pin them in place, curving them into a realistic shape. Sew them on, using either a ladder-stitch around the outside curve, or a zigzag stitch from both sides.

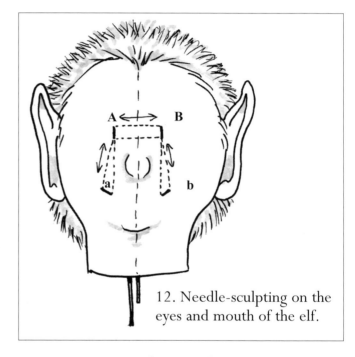

12. Needle-sculpting on the eyes and mouth of the elf.

The Body

Sew the darts closed on the neck and bottom of the body, and then sew the waistline seam on each half, attaching the top to the bottom. The body can now be sewn all the way around, leaving the opening at the back and a small hole at the center of the neck for the head joint. If using very different colors in the top and bottom of the body, try and use matching colors for the sewing threads so that they do not show up when the body is turned and stuffed.

The Limbs

Attach the hands and boots to each arm and leg piece before pinning each entire limb together. You can then sew all around, leaving the opening at the back of each limb. For the leg, the boot sole can then be pinned and stitched into the opening at the bottom of the foot. The toe is the broad part of the sole, and the heel is the narrow part. You will find that the sole fits into the straight bottom of the foot, and does not extend into the pointed toe.

Once the limbs have been sewn and turned, they can be jointed and stuffed. After softly stuffing the hands, you can stitch through each hand to form fingers, as in the pattern piece.

Finishing Details

Once your elf is jointed, stuffed and sewn closed, you can then add finishing details. A leather belt can be made from a strip of leather or Ultrasuede, with an old watch buckle as a belt buckle. Strips of rickrack, chenille yarn, ribbon etc, can be glued to the neck and wrists to form collar and cuffs. If you are making a Santa's helper, you could make his top out of crimson upholstery velvet and add strips of white mohair at the collar and cuffs. Buttons can be sewn down his front, embroidery and beading added to his top and sleeves. His boots can be

decorated with laces, bells on his toes and studs on the soles. He could have a knitted hat or a pointed elf cap, with feathers, bells or a pompon on the tip. Have fun with your accessorizing!

Materials Required:

Ultrasuede, miniature velvet or felt (good in a combination for texture) for all of the following:

Face, ears and hands in flesh tone-
8in x 6in (20cm x 15cm)

Top of body and arms (shirt)-
8in x 8in (20cm x 20cm)

Bottom of body and legs (pants)-
8in x 7in (20cm x 18cm)

Boots- 8in x 6in (20cm x15cm)

Mohair for hair- 5in x 3in (13cm x 8cm)

Eyes-one pair of 5mm black glass.

Joints-10-1in (25mm) discs.

5-cotter pins.

Polyfill stuffing.

Accessories such as buttons, beads, bells, ribbon, chenille, buckles etc.

The Elves' Forest Christmas, made by: (from left to right) Sharolyn Wright, standing elf in pink also by Sharolyn, the author, Leanne Triggs and Wendy Cosford.

Erik Patterns

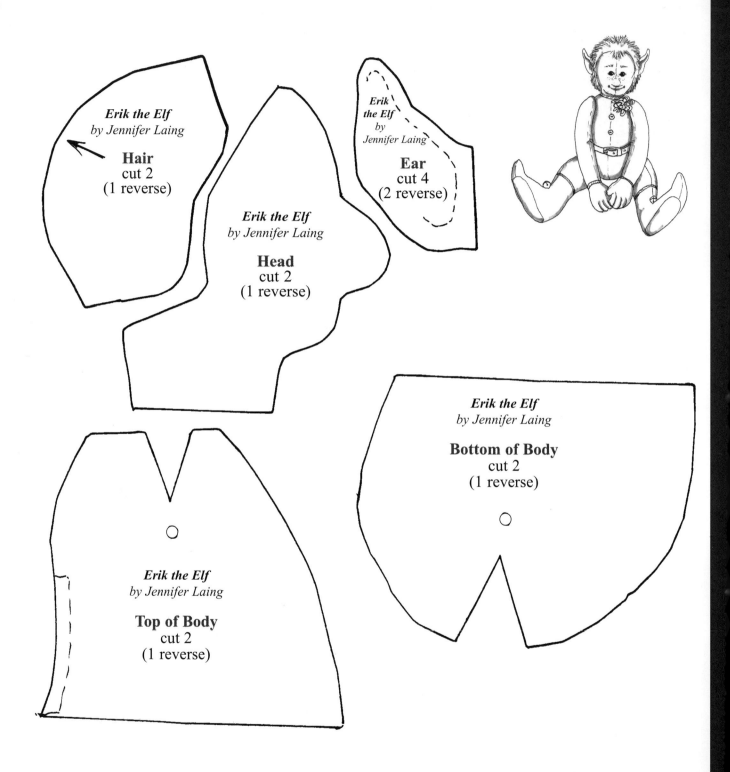

Erik the Elf
by Jennifer Laing

Hair
cut 2
(1 reverse)

Erik the Elf
by Jennifer Laing

Head
cut 2
(1 reverse)

*Erik
the Elf
by
Jennifer Laing*

Ear
cut 4
(2 reverse)

Erik the Elf
by Jennifer Laing

Top of Body
cut 2
(1 reverse)

Erik the Elf
by Jennifer Laing

Bottom of Body
cut 2
(1 reverse)

Erik Patterns

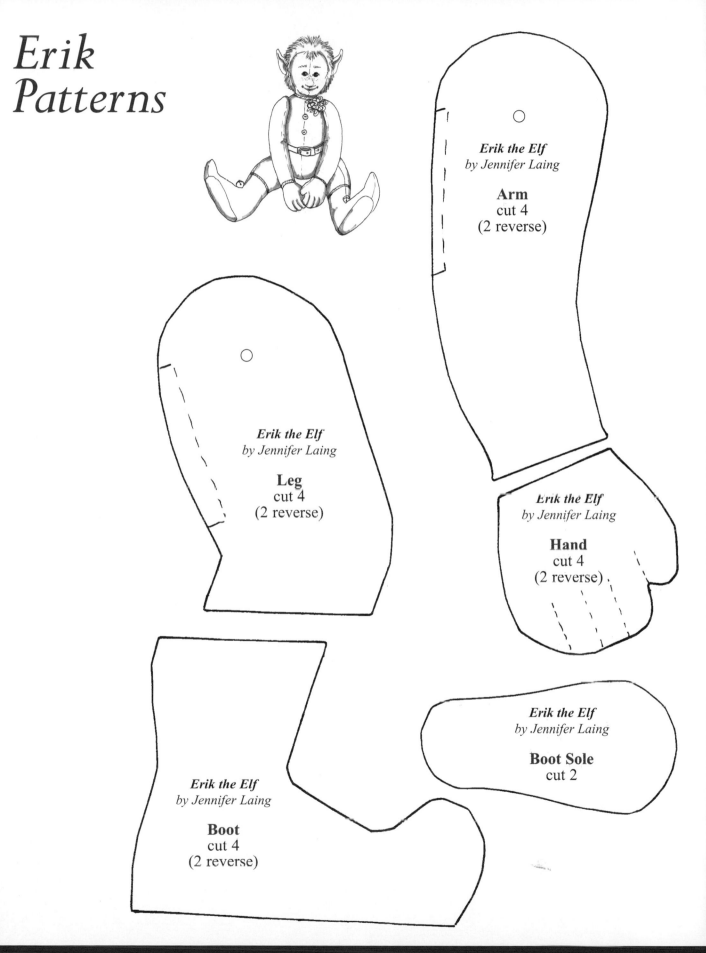

Erik the Elf
by Jennifer Laing

Arm
cut 4
(2 reverse)

Erik the Elf
by Jennifer Laing

Leg
cut 4
(2 reverse)

Erik the Elf
by Jennifer Laing

Hand
cut 4
(2 reverse)

Erik the Elf
by Jennifer Laing

Boot Sole
cut 2

Erik the Elf
by Jennifer Laing

Boot
cut 4
(2 reverse)

Erik the Elf with Nils the Gnome, enjoying a day in the forest.

A gathering of Gnomes, made by: (from left to right) Louise Humphries, Lorraine Falshaw (behind), the author (center), Vicki-Lynn Smith (behind), and Sharolyn Wright.

Nils the Gnome

Nils
An 8in (20cm) Gnome

Nils is a squat little character, and is old and bald. He can be made into a great little Tomten or Santa Claus, just by changing the colors you use to make him up. He can have accessories such as a lumpy, toy-filled sack, a small Christmas wreath or a sprig of mistletoe. He can become a mining gnome with a lamp, shovel and a pile of gemstones, or a forest gnome, collecting berries and nuts. Play around with a selection of colors and textures in felt, upholstery velvet and Ultrasuede until you have a group that go well together. Think about his skin-tone balancing with his hair color, so if he is to have white hair, he might look good with a fair skin-tone. Or he would look good as a tanned weather-beaten gnome with dark skin and grey hair!

The Head

Sew the side or 'ear seam' of each face and back of head together first, and then sew the two halves together around the profile and head. The head can then be turned through and stuffed. Using needle-sculpture, stitch between the eyes to create sockets and lift the corners of the mouth in the same way as for the elf.

The head joint can then be placed in the neck opening and sewn tightly closed, and the eyes can be sewn in, knotting them securely under the edge of the neck. Eyebrows can be tufted in; using the technique detailed earlier in this section, as well as a moustache, and even a comb-over hairstyle! If you want your gnome to have "Friar Tuck" style hair, you can glue a strip of mohair along the back of his head, and also glue on his beard strip under his mouth. Use tacky glue like a rubber cement for this.

Other details like rosy cheeks; lips or wrinkles can be pencilled on with watercolor pencils, or painted on with indelible art marker pens. He could even have eyelids to make him look old and tired, which are easily created out of a tiny semi-circle of flesh-toned Ultrasuede, glued in place half over the eyes.

His ears are made in the same way as for the elf, but are not quite as pointed.

The Body

As with the elf, sew the darts closed first on the body pieces, then sew along the waistband to attach the top to the bottom of each side. Sew the two halves together, leaving the opening at the back and a small opening at the top for the head joint.

The Limbs

Again, these are sewn the same way as the elf's, although the gnome's limbs are much shorter. If you want him to stand, stuff his legs up to the ankles with the finest glass pellets or sand, and then use polyfill for the rest of the limbs and the body.

He can be detailed in the same way as for the elf, and he also has a hat pattern should you wish to make him one. It is simply sewn together down one side of the wedge, and turned through. It can be accessorized with feathers, a bell or a pompon.

Materials Required:

Ultrasuede, miniature velvet or felt (good in combination for texture) for all of the following:

Face, ears and hands in flesh tone- 8in x 6in (20cm x 15cm)

Top of body and arms (Shirt)- 8in x 5in (20cm x 13cm)

Bottom of body and legs (pants)- 8in x 5in (20cm x 13cm)

Boots- 8in x 4in (20cm x 10cm)

Mohair for hair and beard- 4in x 2in (10cm x 5cm)

Hat- 6½in x 4½in (17cm x 12cm)

Eyes- one pair of 5mm black glass.

Joints- 10- 1in/25mm discs.

5-cotter pins.

Polyfill stuffing and fine glass pellets if you want him to be self-standing.

Mohair rovings for tufted eyebrows, hair etc.

Accessories such as buttons, beads, bells, ribbon, chenille, buckles etc.

Nils Patterns

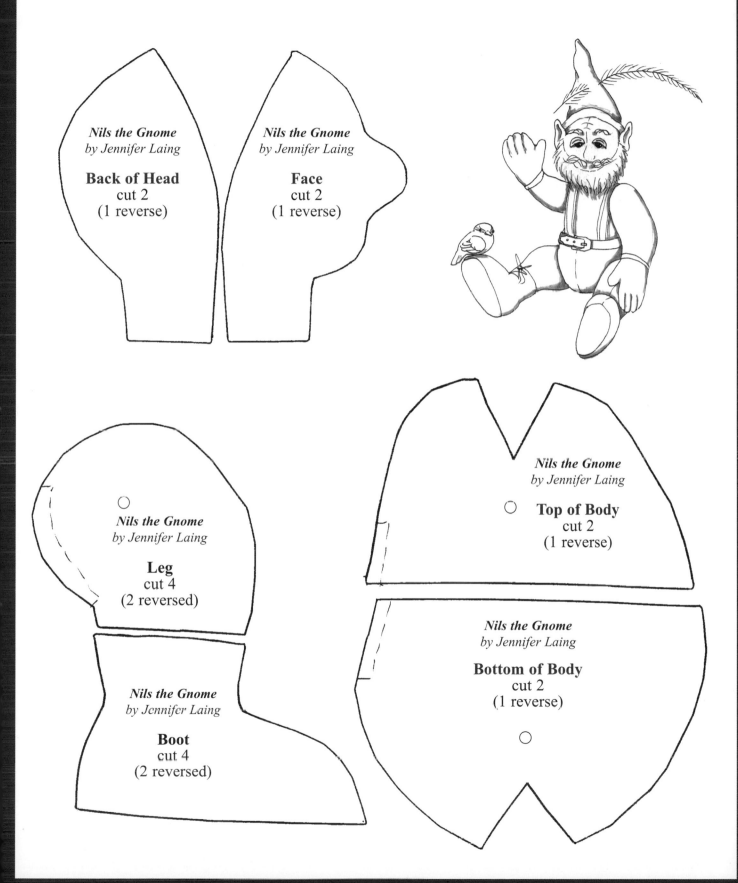

Nils the Gnome
by Jennifer Laing

Back of Head
cut 2
(1 reverse)

Nils the Gnome
by Jennifer Laing

Face
cut 2
(1 reverse)

Nils the Gnome
by Jennifer Laing

Leg
cut 4
(2 reversed)

Nils the Gnome
by Jennifer Laing

Boot
cut 4
(2 reversed)

Nils the Gnome
by Jennifer Laing

Top of Body
cut 2
(1 reverse)

Nils the Gnome
by Jennifer Laing

Bottom of Body
cut 2
(1 reverse)

Nils Patterns

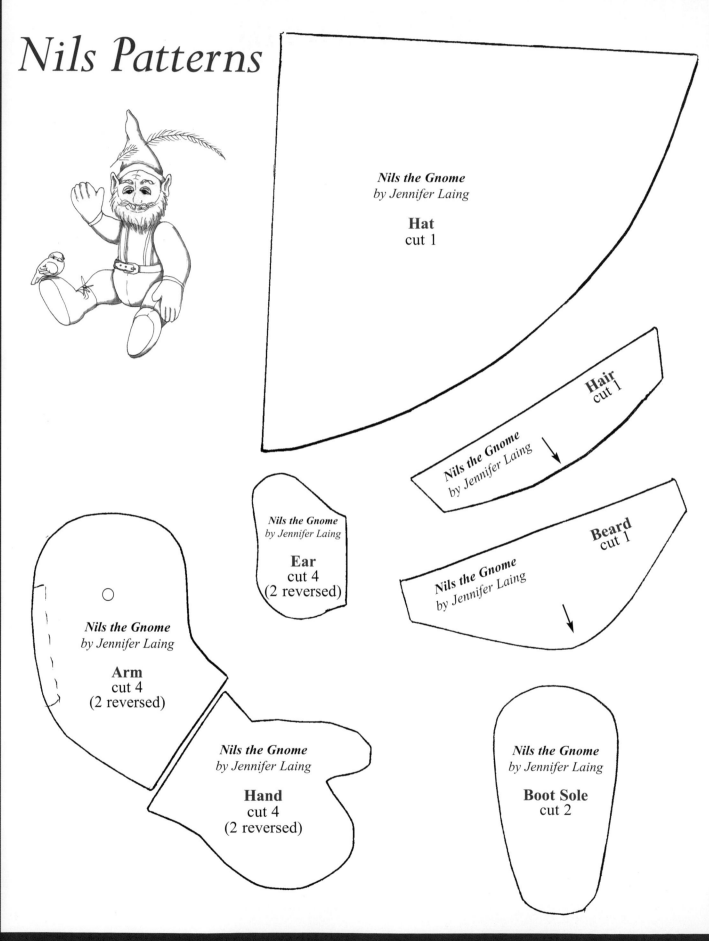

Nils the Gnome
by Jennifer Laing

Hat
cut 1

Nils the Gnome
by Jennifer Laing

Hair
cut 1

Nils the Gnome
by Jennifer Laing

Beard
cut 1

Nils the Gnome
by Jennifer Laing

Ear
cut 4
(2 reversed)

Nils the Gnome
by Jennifer Laing

Arm
cut 4
(2 reversed)

Nils the Gnome
by Jennifer Laing

Hand
cut 4
(2 reversed)

Nils the Gnome
by Jennifer Laing

Boot Sole
cut 2

AMERICA

America has many wonderful animals, but some personal favourites would have to be the bear, and the little pack rat of the Arizona desert. The bear is found in several forms over the North American continent, from the grizzly to the polar bear in the Arctic climates of Canada and Alaska. The pattern for the bear includes a double neck joint, an open mouth, and several variations on pawpad detailing.

Four-legged bears have become popular in recent years, as we turn our attention to the original inspiration for the teddy bear, and also as we become more aware of the plight of real bears in the wild. Many professional bear makers regularly donate part of their annual output for fundraising to help worthwhile charities, and feel a particular affinity for those charities who assist animals.

With the appearance of four-legged bears in the teddy bear world, the artist bear has taken on changes and become more realistic, often incorporating such life-like details as open mouths, teeth, tongues, claws, pawpads and tails.

Ickabod
the Four-Legged Bear

Ickabod the Four-legged Bear, made in alpaca the
color of a rare Kermode or Spirit bear from
British Columbia. He has a waxed template nose
and painted, sculpted pawpads.

Ickabod
A 12in (31cm) Bear

This pattern was one I designed in August 1999, and has been a popular workshop bear in classes I have given around the world. He has been so popular in fact that, due to public demand, the pattern is being included in this book.

Bears and animals with double neck joints are becoming popular, but this is not a new invention. Steiff® first came up with the idea in 1911, for their polar bears. The double neck joint allows extra poseability for a four-legged animal as the extra neck section is an asymmetrical shape. This enables the head to lift up and down as well as swivel. (See Fig.13). When making an ordinary bear or animal, the head is closed at the neck before attaching it to the body. It is the same with a double neck joint, only the closed head is then attached to the neck section. The neck section is then jointed and closed before attaching it to the body. We still work our way from the head to the body, but in this case we have an extra section to include.

As with most realistic animals, they look great when made out of dense "fur" in natural colors. There are some wonderful tipped mohairs available today which make a great grizzly. There are also some fabulous new polar bear shades of ivory on a grey backing, or cream on a darker backing. Making a realistic animal out of sparse mohair can result in something that appears to have the mange, so be careful what you choose!

If you look at real bears you will notice that they have very small eyes, unlike teddy bears. If you want you bear to look more grizzly- or polar-like, try using smaller eyes than you would with a teddy bear of the same size. This pattern is for a 12in (31cm) bear, but he only has little 6mm eyes!

Options

Pawpad details. As this is a more realistic style of bear, and definitely not a teddy, he might look

13. The pose-ability of the double neck joint.

good with some realistic detailing on his pawpads. You can make a stencil of toe details from the pattern if you wish, using the plastic sheets available from patchwork quilt and bear making suppliers. The stencil can be used in a variety of ways:

Painted details can be added, using airbrushing, waterproof paints or waterproof marker pens (available from art supply shops). The marker pens are the cheapest and most user-friendly option. If painting on details, use three shades (a light, medium and dark) to create a three-dimensional effect.

Appliqué details can be added, using the Ultrasuede as the base layer. You might cut out suede, felt, Ultrasuede or leather toe details and glue them in position then stitch around them. If you want to add bulk, just pin them on instead of gluing, and then add a little stuffing behind each toe as you sew it on. This is time consuming, but it is a great effect. If you are making a small bear, such as our Phoebe the Panda, it can get really fiddly trying to make separate appliqué toes. With this pattern we have simplified the toes by making them a single padded strip which we then divide into toes by stitching across the strip.

Trapunto details are also time-consuming, but look equally terrific. Trapunto is a patchwork quilting effect, where the design of the toes is drawn on a piece of scrap fabric, placed on the backside of the Ultrasuede, and then the outlines are stitched through both pieces. Each toe section is then slit on the fabric side, stuffed with a tiny piece of polyfill, and sewn closed. This creates a three-dimensional effect on the front side.

All the three above ideas are created on the flat footpads, before sewing the pads onto the leg.

Sculpted toes or pulled toes. For another, and perhaps faster idea, you can sew in the plain footpads, and stuff them to the ankle. You can then create "pulled toes" with needle sculpture. This technique was outlined in my last book Teddy Bear Art, but Fig.14 will show you an improved

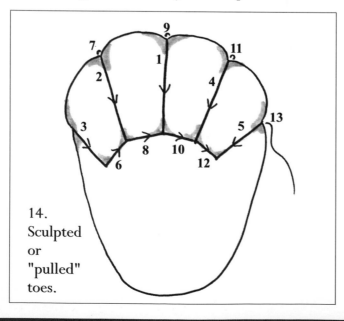

14. Sculpted or "pulled" toes.

method. Ultrasuede is the best fabric to use for this, as is has a bit of stretch. Felt tends to crumple more easily.

The important tips are; get your stuffing even, firm yet springy, and pay particular attention to the seam edge around the toes. Use strong upholstery thread (used single, not double) that matches your pawpad color. Always start from the edge of your fur and fabric seam, and stitch into the pawpad. Pull firmly from your first stitch, and keep the tension while making all your stitches. The stitches need to be fairly wide at the top and angle into the pad in order to create the toe effect. Hold up your hand with your fingers spread as wide as you can. That is the line of your stitches!

The illustration shows just one way of making toes, with five stitches creating four toe pads. You might want to make less or more toes, make the bottom line straight instead of curved, make the stitches shorter and the toes smaller etc. You can also shade in your finished toes with your waterproof markers or other paints, for a very realistic look.

Inset Chest/Muzzle

This is another area where you have an option to be a little more creative. You might wish to inset a lighter or darker fur into the muzzle and or chest area. You will only need a scrap of mohair for this, and it need not be in the same style or length of mohair in order to work well. A brown or black grizzly bear looks great with an inset muzzle and chest of gold or tan, and a polar bear looks realistic with a muzzle inset with grey. Alternatively, you might like to make an Ultrasuede muzzle, which looks wonderful on a grizzly and really enhances needle sculpting on the face.

On your pattern sheets you will see lines for the inset pieces on the head and body. Allow the seam allowance each side (i.e. the dotted lines) when cutting out. To alter the marked out pieces, you can easily cut off the chest from the body, and the nose from the head sides and gusset, allowing a ¼in (.65cm) seam allowance. Then make a pattern piece for the inset chest and nose pieces (allowing that extra ¼in [.65cm] seam) for your second color of mohair or Ultrasuede. Sew the new pieces onto the existing head and body pieces in order to create your original outline, before making up the head and body as usual.

Sewing the Head and Open Mouth

The head is a normal three-piece pattern, but with an open mouth. There are several ways to create an open mouth, but this is probably the easiest. The side head pieces are sewn together as usual, from the point of the nose down to the front edge of the neck, but in this case leaving the slit for the mouth open (Fig. 15).

Before the gusset is sewn in, the mouth lining is attached. Possibly the tricky bits like sewing in the open mouth are best tackled by hand. This is done simply by opening out the mouth slit until it is flattened out, rather like the foot on a leg pattern. The mouth lining is then sewn in just like a footpad (Fig. 16). Pin it in first at the two seams you have just created in the head, at the top and bottom jaw edges. Then pin in the corners of the mouth at the sides, and finally place in more pins around the gaps to make it easy to sew without puckering. Make sure that the lining is sewn in longways and not sideways, that is, the longest part is from upper seam to lower seam, and the narrowest part is in the corners of the mouth (where it folds when the mouth is shut). If the fabric corners of the mouth look a little weak, you can put a spot of glue there (watered-down PVA or Craft Glue is best) to protect the edges. Fray-Check can be a little stiff.

Once the mouth lining is sewn in, sew in the gusset as normal. Before turning the head through, pin on one of the four mohair discs, and sew it on halfway around (Fig. 17). Turn the head through, place in the head joint (bolt, washer and disc) and then stuff the head. It is important to place in the joint at this stage, otherwise it will be difficult to put in the joint after the head is stuffed.

Sewing the neck section. Sew the short sides of the neckband together first, making a loop. Then sew on a disc of mohair on the side with the fur facing inward, that is, away from the edge. Finish by sewing on another disc on the side with the fur facing outwards, but only sew this disc on halfway

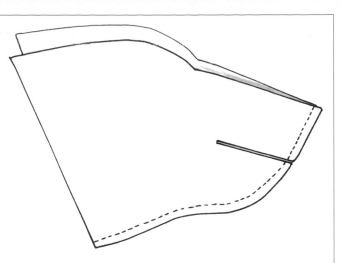

15. The first seams sewn on the head of an open-mouthed bear or animal.

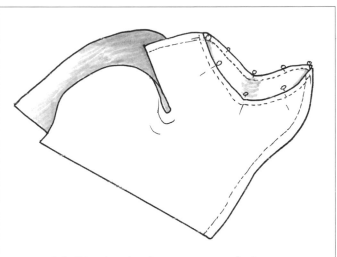

16. Pinning in the open mouthpiece.

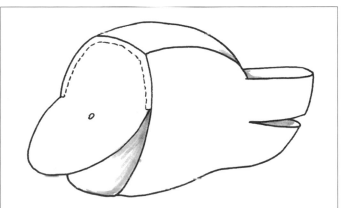

17. Adding the first circle on the back of the head.

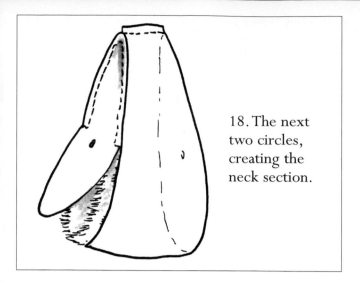

18. The next two circles, creating the neck section.

around. We now have a little round box with a lid (Fig. 18).

The reason we use discs of mohair instead of gathering, is to avoid the snowman effect, that is the look of a smaller ball (the head) on a larger ball (the body). As this is a more realistic style of bear, we want the look of a strong head on a thick neck and onto a stronger body. By adding discs of mohair between the discs instead of gathering, we avoid bulges and create a sleeker look. The discs are only slightly smaller than the openings, which means that the seams will be under the finished edges between the joints and invisible in the finished bear.

The body is a simple two-part pattern, but with darts at the bottom to enhance a more rounded behind. The opening for the body is at the tummy, and the neck opening is capped with the fourth of the mohair discs (Fig. 19).

The legs are straight on the front ones and slightly bent on the back ones, but all the pads are the same size, allowing for four footpads the same size. Remember to detail your pads first before sewing them in, unless you want to try the pulled toes. Also remember that the feet are designed with the toes as the widest part, in order to allow room for pawpad detailing.

The tail is rather like an ear, but with a short and a long side. Simply sew along the outer curve, like an ear, and turn through. Do not edge the rough edges, or sew it closed, merely place a small piece

of stuffing inside it. When your bear is completed, stuffed and closed, the tail can be attached. Stand the bear up and look at him in profile. You want the tail to sit on the curve of his bottom, just below the top line of the spine. Looking at the bear from behind, the tail will be positioned between the tops of his legs, and most likely will cover the body darts. With the stuffing inside the tail, tuck the raw edges of the tail under with your fingers, and pin it on in an open, oval shape. You will find that the pin underneath the tail will pull it down so that it sits at a natural angle, tucked down on the body. The tail can then be ladder-stitched on.

Shading the Face and Paws

Using indelible or permanent ink art pens, you can shade your bear quite realistically. Look at photos of real bears and see where color changes occur. There might be a dark smudge around their eyes, especially in the inner corner of their eyes where the fur is moist. The fur might look darker around the tip of the nose where the fur is shorter and the dark skin shows through. This is especially true on polar bears, where their black skin shows through their fur, giving shades of grey where the fur gets shorter.

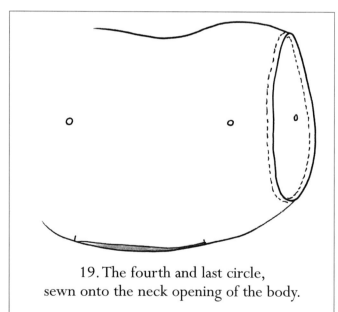

19. The fourth and last circle, sewn onto the neck opening of the body.

If you are using two colors of mohair on your bear, and have inset a muzzle or chest, you can use colored pens to blend the two colors together and blur the transition line. You can also use color to create a shape where it was too tricky to actually sew in a second color, for example, a small panda's eye patches. Color can also be used on the pawpads, to create the look of pads by drawing them on, or by shading around the shapes you might have already created with needle-sculpting or appliquéing.

The Template or Built-Up Nose

If you want to create a bulbous nose, there are several ways to achieve this. You can build up layers of stitches till you get the bulk you want, you can make a nose out of leather or Ultrasuede (see the koala pattern), or you can use a template as a base and then stitch over it to create a three-dimensional nose.

If you want to try this template style nose, you will first have to ensure that the stuffing in the muzzle area is firm. The stitches used in this type of nose are much tighter than in a normal nose, and may distort the muzzle if it is not firmly packed. Then cut a shape out of leather or thick Ultrasuede the width of your stuffed head's muzzle, as seen in Fig. 20. If the leather or Ultrasuede is fine you can stick a couple of layers together, using a tacky glue or rubber cement. You can then pare down the edges to thin them a little, using sharp scissors at an angle.

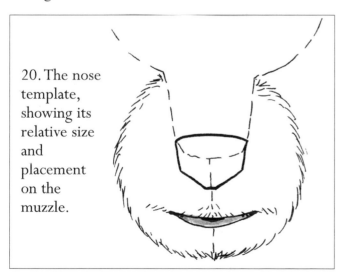

20. The nose template, showing its relative size and placement on the muzzle.

The template works best when it is a simple square shape as illustrated. The stitches will tend to slip off a fancy, curved shape, or distort very small pointed parts of a complicated template outline. If you are planning on making a fancy shaped nose, you can still use a template to provide central

bulk, but then extend your stitching to include the extra design beyond the border of your template.

Glue the template in place, making sure that it is centerd and covers the T-seam at the end of the muzzle. This will ensure that your needle will not have to go through the tough seams as you stitch the nose. Using a double thread (DMC#5 is a good thickness for this sized bear) on a 3in-5in doll needle with a knot on the end, start at the neck and bring the thread up to where you wish to start.

The nose is usually started with the center stitch, and may include the septum stitch, or have that as a separate stitch after the nose is completed. See Fig. 21 for details. The main things to remember with using a template are:
* keep your stitches away from the edge of the template, so as not to roll the template under and lose its' shape.
* keep your stitches tight. The tightness of your stitches is what makes the template compress down and creates the curve and three-dimensional shape of this type of nose. Your stitches should be tight enough so that they do not shift or slip, even when rubbed over with your finger.
* make sure your stitches get even tighter as you get to the sides. Increase the tension for each of your stitches for the outer third of each side of the nose. This will create the curved side shapes for the nose, and also ensure that you do not have any bulk left at the sides of the template for the stitches to slip off. The stitches should be pulled so tight by the time that you reach the side edge of the

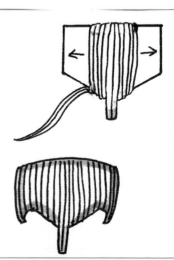

21. How to stitch over the template, avoiding the edges and tightening the stitches towards the outer edges.

template, the stitches are just about flush with the fabric, and cover the edges of the template.

A Waxed Nose

Any stitched nose can be waxed over to give it a shine, but not every nose looks good waxed and shiny. You must think about whether or not this will suit your bear. While it may bring a realistic bear to life, a shiny wet-look nose might not be appropriate for a worn, antique-style bear.

There are many different materials you can use to create a shiny nose, from industrial polishes and varnishes to fabric craft dimensional fabric paints, glues which leave a shiny finish, melted and polished beeswax, craft waxes and shoe polishes. The glues and fabric paints will make the nose shiny but will not hide any bumpy stitches. The waxes and polishes, however, because they have to be buffed with a brush, or a piece of paper or plastic, will often meld the stitches together more, and smooth out any irregularities. Experiment with different mediums and see which you feel most comfortable using.

Even with a single type of material, such as beeswax, there are many different techniques you can use to apply it. You can melt beeswax in a microwave, paint it on while wet and steaming hot, then buff it with an old toothbrush or even a piece of thin cardboard or paper. You can soften beeswax in a double boiler and spread it on the nose like butter, before polishing it. You can use a softer form of beeswax, and mold it directly onto the nose, then melt it in with a hairdryer and polish it. You can rub the beeswax directly into the nose and then polish it with a hot knife. You can build up layers of beeswax until you have a perfectly smooth nose like leather, or you can just put a single, light layer of wax on the nose to give it a shine, but so you can still see the texture of the stitching underneath.

Claws

Claws can be added for a more realistic effect, and can be made out of a variety of materials including Fimo and leather. Often the hard claws made out of baked materials such as Fimo can be rather delicate and are liable to breakage over time. A softer, more flexible material such as leather will last longer.

Leather claws can be cut out in a long diamond shape (do it folded in half for a perfectly symmetrical shape), as in Fig. 22A. Then, fold them in half and stretch the folded edge, giving the claw a realistic, curved-down shape. Each leather claw can then be stitched on to the end of the stuffed foot.

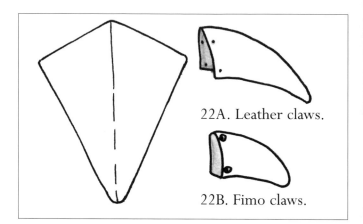

22A. Leather claws.

22B. Fimo claws.

If you desire hard claws, then form Fimo shapes in the size you want, and poke a hole through the end of each claw, as in Fig. 22B. Bake it following the instructions on your Fimo or other brand of modelling clay's packet. If the finished claws are dull and you want them shiny, you can varnish them with craft varnish or even with clear nail polish. The finished claws can then be stitched into position on the end of the stuffed feet, using the holes in the claws like buttons.

Materials Required

¼ yard or meter of ½in (1cm) pile mohair.
  (You will have some left over if you mark it out economically, but it will take a bit more than an ⅛ of a yard.)
12in x 2½in (30cm x 6cm) of Ultrasuede for pawpads
Scrap of pinkish Ultrasuede for mouth lining
12 -1½in/40mm joint discs
6 - bolts and 4 - locknuts, 2 ordinary nuts; OR 6 - cotter pins; OR 2 - cotter pins and 4 -locknuts and bolts.
1 pair of 6mm glass eyes.
DMC#5 for nose and claws
Scrap of Ultrasuede or leather for nose template
Polyfill, pellets
Material for pawpad appliqué if desired.

A scrum of Ickabods, showing their very different faces, made by: (from left to right) Vicki-Lynn Smith, Sharolyn Wright, the author and Susan Carroll.

Ickabod Patterns

Ickabod the Bear
by Jennifer Laing

Body
cut 2
(1 reverse)

Ickabod the Bear
by Jennifer Laing

Neck Collar
cut 1

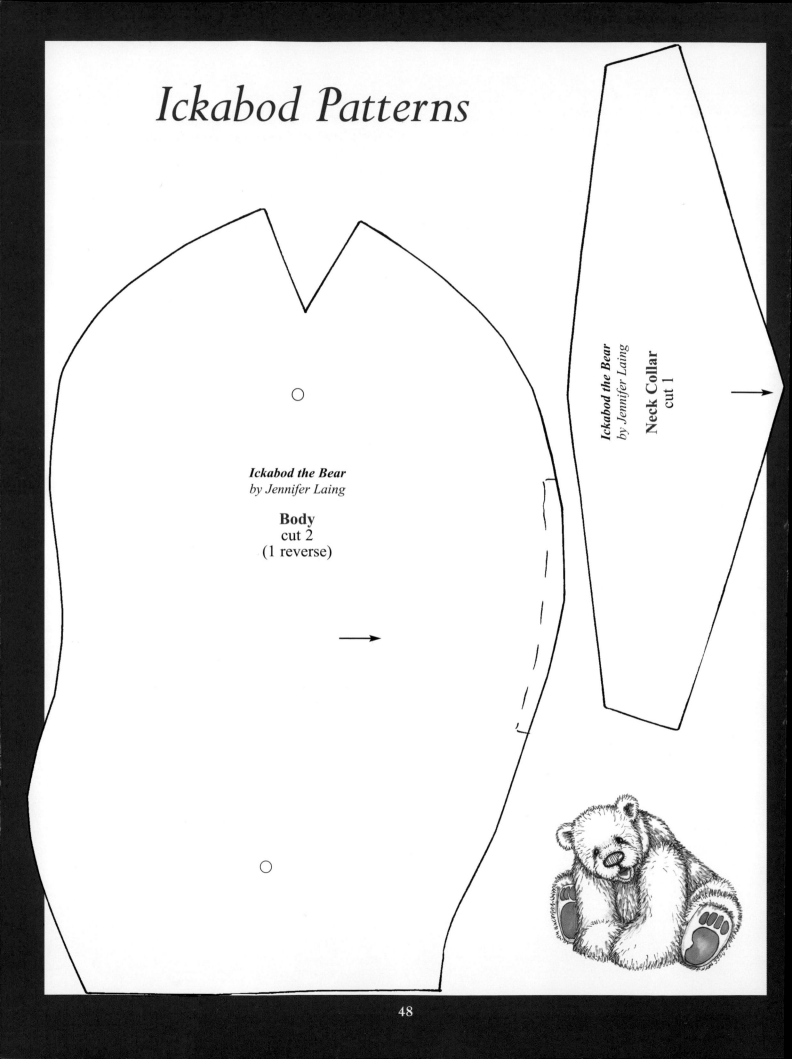

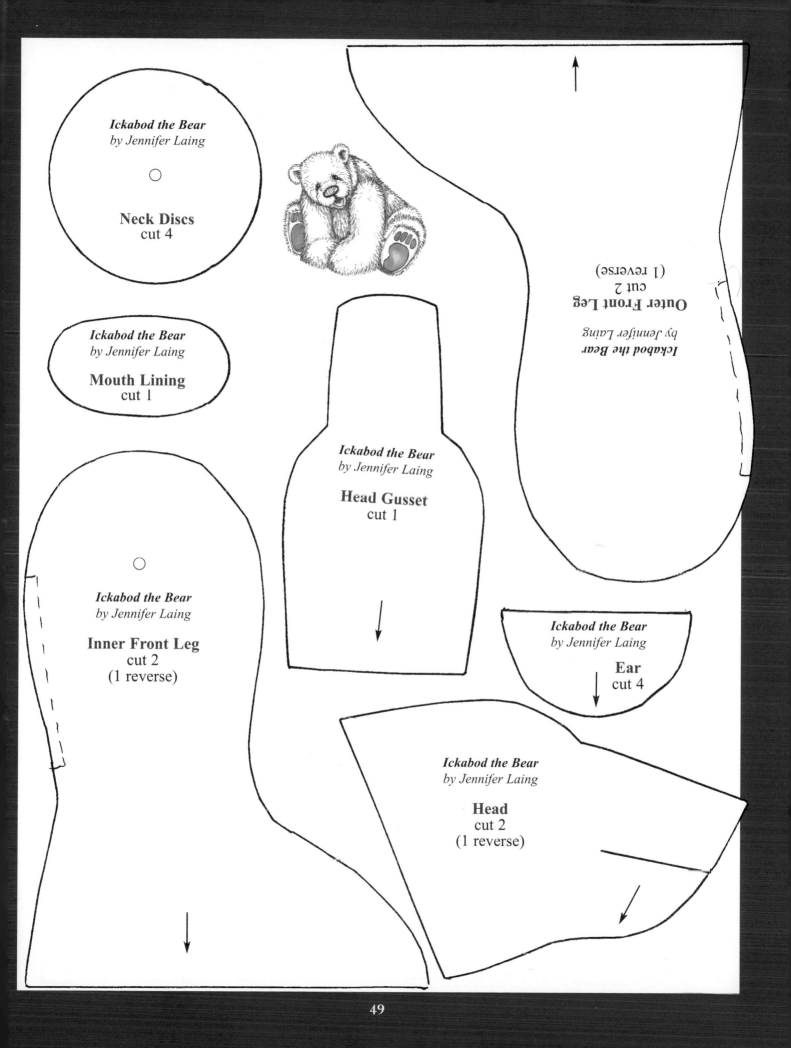

Ickabod the Bear
by Jennifer Laing

Neck Discs
cut 4

Ickabod the Bear
by Jennifer Laing

Mouth Lining
cut 1

Ickabod the Bear
by Jennifer Laing

Inner Front Leg
cut 2
(1 reverse)

Ickabod the Bear
by Jennifer Laing

Head Gusset
cut 1

(1 reverse)
cut 2
Outer Front Leg
by Jennifer Laing
Ickabod the Bear

Ickabod the Bear
by Jennifer Laing

Ear
cut 4

Ickabod the Bear
by Jennifer Laing

Head
cut 2
(1 reverse)

49

Ickabod Patterns

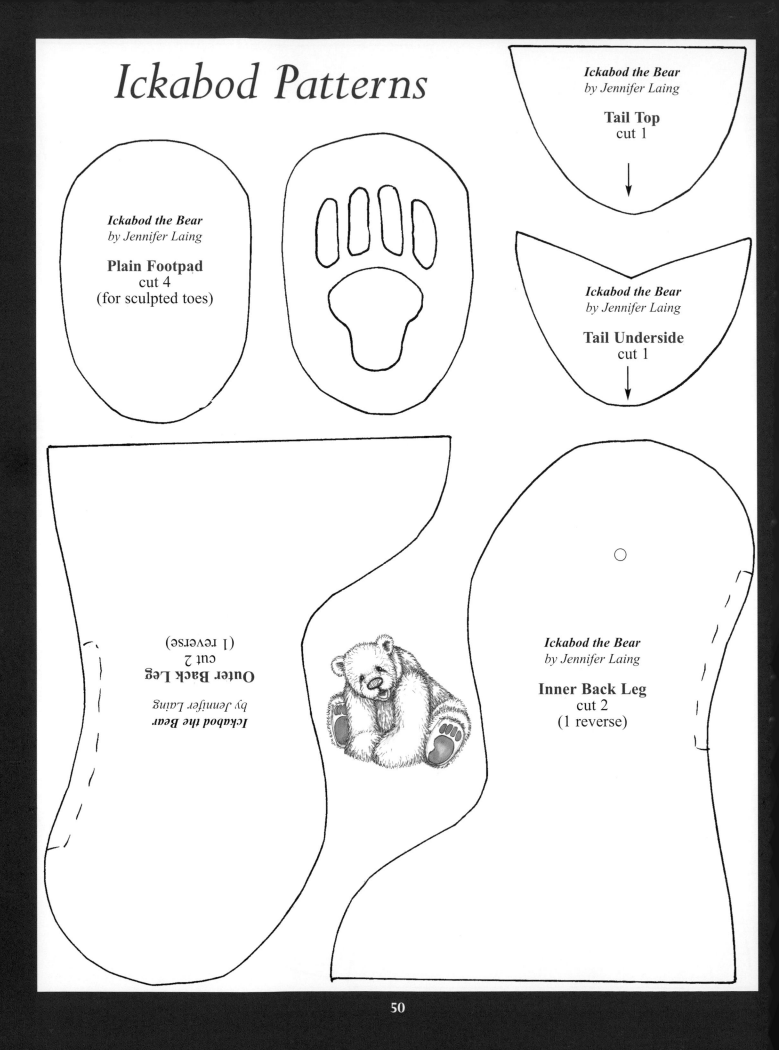

Ickabod the Bear
by Jennifer Laing

Tail Top
cut 1

Ickabod the Bear
by Jennifer Laing

Plain Footpad
cut 4
(for sculpted toes)

Ickabod the Bear
by Jennifer Laing

Tail Underside
cut 1

Outer Back Leg
cut 2
(1 reverse)

Ickabod the Bear
by Jennifer Laing

Ickabod the Bear
by Jennifer Laing

Inner Back Leg
cut 2
(1 reverse)

Tom Collins
the Pack Rat

Tom Collins the Pack Rat, in the Southwestern desert, with his backpack (containing all sorts of found treasure, including a miniature Barbie® doll!)

Tom Collins
A 7in (18cm) Pack Rat

Being a rodent lover, and having kept fancy mice and hooded rats as pets (rats are smart, clean and very sweet!), I naturally fell in love with the pack rat as soon as I learned about him when I was a child. He is a native of the desert, collecting the local flora to make his cool burrow more comfortable. Interesting, but seemingly useless objects he finds are also taken home. People who tend to hoard things are sometimes called pack rats! I prefer to think of pack rats as animal interior designers, the bower birds of the rodent world.

My dear friend Bonnie Windell, who also happens to be one of the USA's top bear artists, designs and makes the best rats and mice I have ever seen. I have several in my collection, and this little Pack Rat in no way competes with them. Bonnie is a fellow rat-lover, and we both bemoan the fact that our spouses hate rats. In fact, my partner's whole family hates them so much, I just had to lovingly name this one after them in the hopes that it will soften their feelings towards small rodents!

Tom Collins the pack rat is made of mohair and Ultrasuede, but as he is small he does not use up much of either fabric. As rodents such as mice and rats have fine, clever fingers and toes with little hair on them, his paws and feet are made of Ultrasuede from the elbows and knees down. He has cotter pin joints and small glass pellets weighting his back legs and enabling him to stand unaided. He has a pipe cleaner in his tail for flexibility, and horsehair whiskers, which are securely tufted in. His ears are a single layer of Ultrasuede, allowing them to be thin and supple, just like the real animal. There is shading on the inside of his ears, and around his eyes to give him extra character. His toes on both his hands and feet are sculpted with some simple stitches.

Sewing the Head

Unlike your standard pattern, where the side head pieces are first sewn together from the tip of the nose down to the neck edge, and then the gusset is sewn-in, this pattern works best when sewn together differently. This is because there is no definite tip to the nose, instead it slopes down and is round at the end, giving it a softer, more pointed shape suitable for a little rat or mouse. As there is no easy to use spot to judge where the nose point of the gusset fits into the tip of the nose on the side head pieces, it is actually easier to sew it in backwards. That is, sewing in the gusset before sewing the side head pieces together under the nose.

Place your first pin at the back edge of the head, pinning together the bottom edge of the gusset to the back of the side head piece. Work your way forward, pinning the gusset to the side head piece until you reach the nose end of the gusset. Repeat on the other side with the other side head piece, and make sure that the point of the nose is evenly situated on both sides. The head can then be sewn, and finished off with the seam under the nose down to the front of the neck.

Placing of Ears

The large ears can be subtly colored with flesh shaded art pens, and then pinned in a curved shape, using the gusset seam as your starting point for the top edge. The ears can then be ladder-stitched in place.

Nose Stitching

This is very easy, and just requires DMC#5 floss in flesh pink. You can start and finish the thread at the base of the neck, as close to the joint disc as possible. If this is done before the head is jointed to the body, then your thread can be easily hidden under the neck. Using a double strand, make a fly stitch, along the gusset seams as in Fig. 23 and form the mouth the same way, making the mouth stitch long enough to give him a subtle smile. The rabbit's mouth is precisely the same.

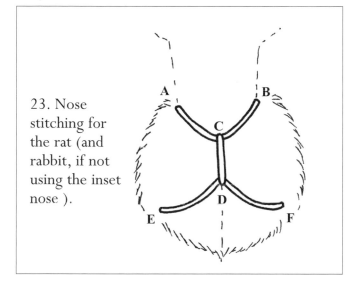

23. Nose stitching for the rat (and rabbit, if not using the inset nose).

Needle-Sculpting For Eye Sockets

Before placing in the eyes, stitch between the eyes using a strong thread and pull to indent the sockets. Start and finish your thread from the edge of the neck.

Tufted Whiskers

Use horsehair for the whiskers if you can, as it is much softer and more realistic than either floss or fishing line. Follow the instructions in the Elf and Gnome section for how to tuft.

Stitching of Toes and Claws

Using your strong upholstery thread, create four little toes with three stitches right through the foot, as in Fig. 24A. If making the toes while the leg is still open, you can bring your needle through the opening with a knot on the end to start, then finish by knotting over the top of a stitch and pulling it inside. The claws are created in the same way as the toes, as in Fig. 24B.

Sewing the Tail

This is a long, narrow piece of Ultrasuede. If you think you may have difficulty turning it through, or do not have a hemostat for turning, you can just as easily sew it entirely with ladder-stitch from the outside. Once it is right-side-out, place a pipe cleaner inside with the end protruding about ½in (1cm) or a centimeter. Pour some fine glass beads into the tail (you can do this without a pipe cleaner if you like, for a different effect) and top with a piece of polyfill to hold the beads in around the pipe cleaner.

Once the body has been jointed and stuffed, position the tail and poke a small hole there with an awl to take the end of the pipe cleaner sticking out of the tail. Push in the pipe cleaner; pin the tail on in an open rounded shape and ladder-stitch it in place.

Materials Required

Mohair- a 10in x 8in piece (26cm x 20cm) with a ¼in (65cm) pile.
Ultrasuede- a 6in x 6in piece (15cm x 15cm)
Joints- 5-mini T-pins.
   2-19mm discs for the head
   4-13mm discs for the arms
   4-25mm discs for the legs
Nose and mouth- DMC #5 in a skin-tone color.
Eyes- 5mm glass.
Pipe cleaner for inside the tail.
Long horsehair for the whiskers.
Polyfill stuffing.
Fine glass pellets for the feet and lower legs.

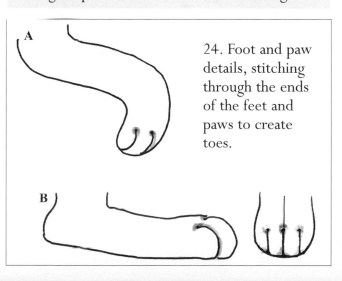

24. Foot and paw details, stitching through the ends of the feet and paws to create toes.

The Rat Pack, made in mohair and alpaca by: (from left to right) Susan Carroll, Julie Blake, the author, Wendy Cosford and Vicki-Lynn Smith. There are also some stone Zuni fetishes from New Mexico in the photo, the rattlesnake by Kent Banteah and the frog by Ricky Laahty.

Tom Collins Patterns

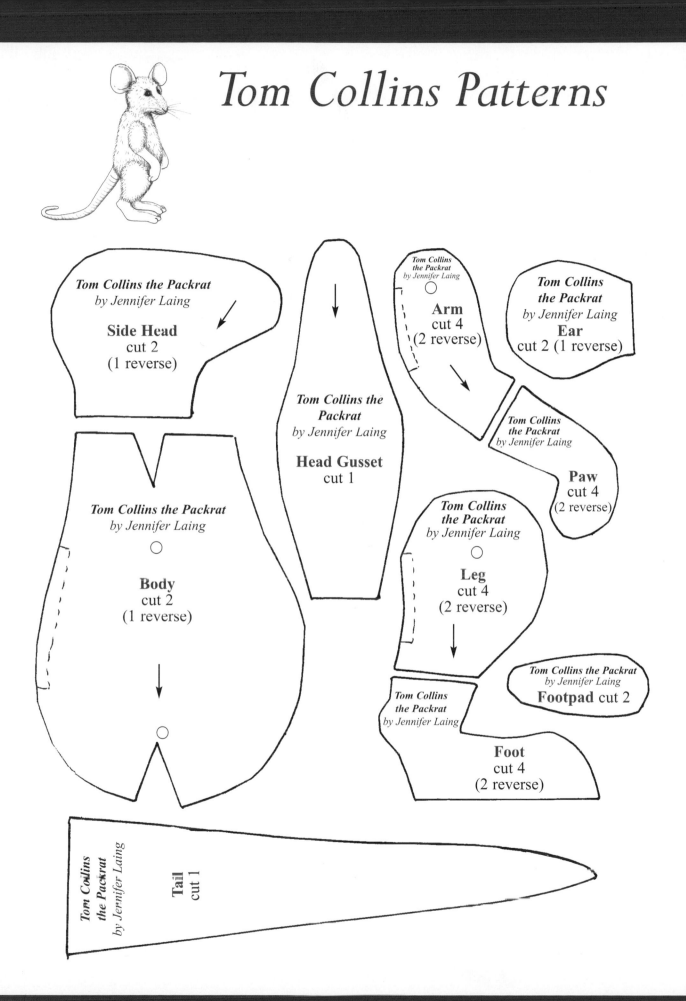

Tom Collins the Packrat
by Jennifer Laing

Side Head
cut 2
(1 reverse)

Tom Collins the
Packrat
by Jennifer Laing

Head Gusset
cut 1

Tom Collins
the Packrat
by Jennifer Laing

Arm
cut 4
(2 reverse)

Tom Collins
the Packrat
by Jennifer Laing
Ear
cut 2 (1 reverse)

Tom Collins
the Packrat
by Jennifer Laing

Paw
cut 4
(2 reverse)

Tom Collins the Packrat
by Jennifer Laing

Body
cut 2
(1 reverse)

Tom Collins
the Packrat
by Jennifer Laing

Leg
cut 4
(2 reverse)

Tom Collins the Packrat
by Jennifer Laing

Footpad cut 2

Tom Collins
the Packrat
by Jennifer Laing

Foot
cut 4
(2 reverse)

Tom Collins
the Packrat
by Jennifer Laing

Tail
cut 1

Africa

Having just returned from my first African safari, I was awed by the variety and amount of wildlife living in the game parks. It was late spring, the vegetation was lush and green, and all the animals had young ones with them. Some of my favorites were the monkeys and the elephants. The vervet monkeys had their babies clinging to the mothers' tummies, while the elephants herded their little ones protectively in the middle of their maternal group.

Esme the Elephant

Esme
A little 5½in (14cm) Elephant

Elephants look great when they are made out of grey wool felt, Ultrasuede, upholstery velvet or even thin leather. I have even seen them created out of canvas, which is then painted like oilcloth to look like elephant hide. You could even make this pattern into a woolly mammoth by using reddish mohair and giving it tusks.

Esme is just a baby elephant, so she doesn't have tusks yet. If you want to create tusks however, you can easily make some out of two long curved; wedge-shaped piece of ivory colored Ultrasuede. Sew these up to create two long cone shapes, stuff them and bend them slightly and then insert them into the cheeks, near the mouth edges, by making a small slit on each side. They can be glued in or stitched in place.

Esme has a wired trunk, using a pipe cleaner, and has sculpted wrinkles, and eyelids. Her tail has a horsehair tuft on the end, and she has shading to outline her wrinkles and toes. She is an African elephant so she has large ears, but if you prefer you can cut the ears down in size to create an Asian elephant instead. If you want to create a circus elephant with a ruff and a tub to stand on, it would be an Asian elephant, as African elephants are rarely tamed for circuses.

Sewing the Head and Trunk

The trunk is three-sided, with the underside sewn to the lower edge of the two side head pieces. The first thing, however, is to sew the mouth lining to the widest end of the trunk underside, as in Fig. 25. This strip is then sewn to each head side piece, with the mouth lining folding back to reach the tip of the bottom lip, also shown in Fig. 25.

The gusset is then sewn-in, starting from the neck edge at the back of the head and working forward. Where the gusset point finishes, the two side trunk pieces are sewn together down to the tip of the trunk. The tiny triangular trunk tip is sewn-in last, and one of the two circles is sewn halfway around the neck opening. The head is turned through, a pipe cleaner folded in half is inserted into the trunk and the head is stuffed. The joint should be placed in the head (with the joint shaft passing through the center of the circle in the neck) before stuffing, as it will be hard to get it in place after the head is filled.

Needle-Sculpting the Eyes, Mouth and Wrinkles

Needle-sculpting can take place before the neck is closed, with the needle and thread coming up through the open neck. Stitch between the eyes to form sockets, then stitch from one eye socket down to the center of the throat and back up to the other eye socket. Pull to create a deepened throat, as in Fig. 26A. Stitch again from one eye socket, this time down to the corner of the mouth, and pull up to the other eye socket. Do this again for the other side of the mouth, and you will create a smile by lifting the corners of the mouth.

To create wrinkles, form a type of ladder-stitch as in Fig. 27B, with at least a ¼in (.65cm) gap between your rows of stitches. This will allow enough fabric to be bunched up when the stitches are pulled, creating wrinkles. Try a couple of rows of wrinkles up the trunk, and even a stitch into the end of the trunk pulled up to the wrinkles in order to deepen the trunk opening. He can also have wrinkles on his forehead, and around each knee and elbow, ankle etc. He can be as baggy as you like!

Placing In the Eyes and Adding the Eyelids

The eyes can be sewn-in, pulled firmly to the base of the neck, and knotted off there. If this is done before the head is attached to the body, there will be no visible knot on the finished head. Eyelids can be cut as semicircles from scraps of your fabric, and glued halfway over the eyes with tacky glue. You could even add a thin strip of mohair for eyelashes if you like, gluing them to the underside of the eyelid before attaching it to the eye. Elephants do have lovely, long eyelashes!

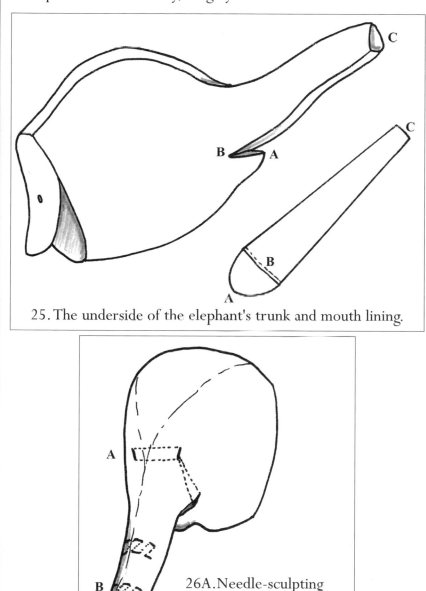

25. The underside of the elephant's trunk and mouth lining.

26A. Needle-sculpting the elephant's eye sockets and mouth.
26B. Needle-sculpting wrinkles on the elephant's trunk.

The Ears

If you are using wool felt or Ultrasuede, you may want to have the ears as a single thickness of fabric. Upholstery velvet only has one side, however, so you will have to cut two opposing pieces for each ear and glue or sew them together. The ears are pinned on fairly flat, but with a slight curve at the top edge. They should be able to be pushed back flat or pulled away from the head, so that they look quite lifelike in their positioning. Ladder-stitch them in place, and knot under the edge of the ear.

The Body

The darts are sewn up on each body half and then the two halves are sewn together, leaving the opening at the tummy and also leaving the neck edge unsewn. The second of the two circles is then used to sew around the neck and close it off. The body can then be turned through.

The Limbs

The four legs of the elephant are sewn up, leaving the opening at the back of each limb, and sewing on the round footpads at the bottom of each limb. They can then be turned through, jointed and stuffed. Toenails can be added, either by painting them on with an indelible art marker, using white puff paint for fabric, or embroidering them on.

Making the Tail

The tail is ladder-stitched into a tube, leaving the curved edge open at the top. A tuft of hair can be added by using a strip of mohair, the tip of an old or cheap paintbrush, or a tuft of horsehair. Place a spot of tacky glue on the base of your hair, and poke it into the end of the tail, using a sauté skewer or other fine pointed object.

Once your elephant is stuffed, jointed and closed, stand him up and position his tail in the most natural spot. Pin it, then ladder-stitch it in place.

Materials Required

Ultrasuede, miniature bear velvet or wool felt in grey - 18in x 12in (46cm x 31cm)
Joints - 10 - 1¼in (3cm) 30mm discs.
5 - mini T-shaped cotter pins.
Eyes - 4mm black glass.
Polyfill stuffing.
Pipe cleaner for the trunk.
Hair for the eyelashes and tail tuft.

Esme Patterns

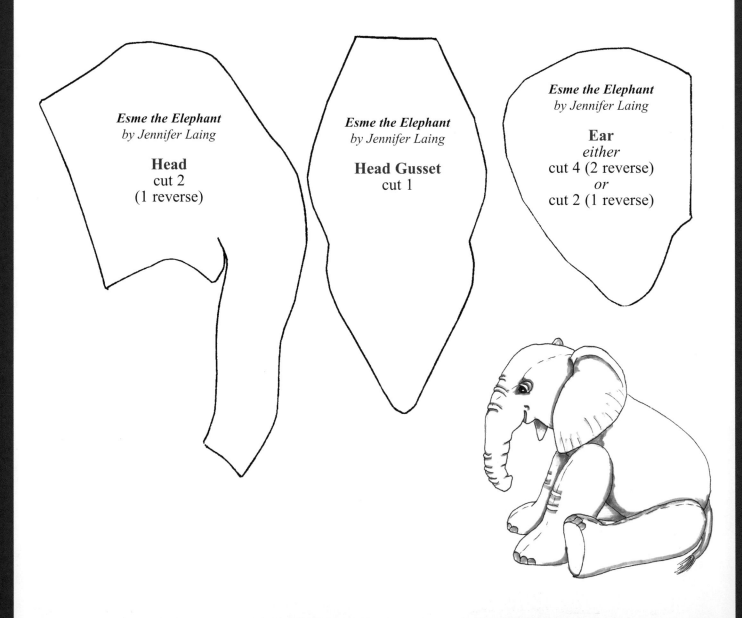

Esme the Elephant
by Jennifer Laing

Head
cut 2
(1 reverse)

Esme the Elephant
by Jennifer Laing

Head Gusset
cut 1

Esme the Elephant
by Jennifer Laing

Ear
either
cut 4 (2 reverse)
or
cut 2 (1 reverse)

Esme Patterns

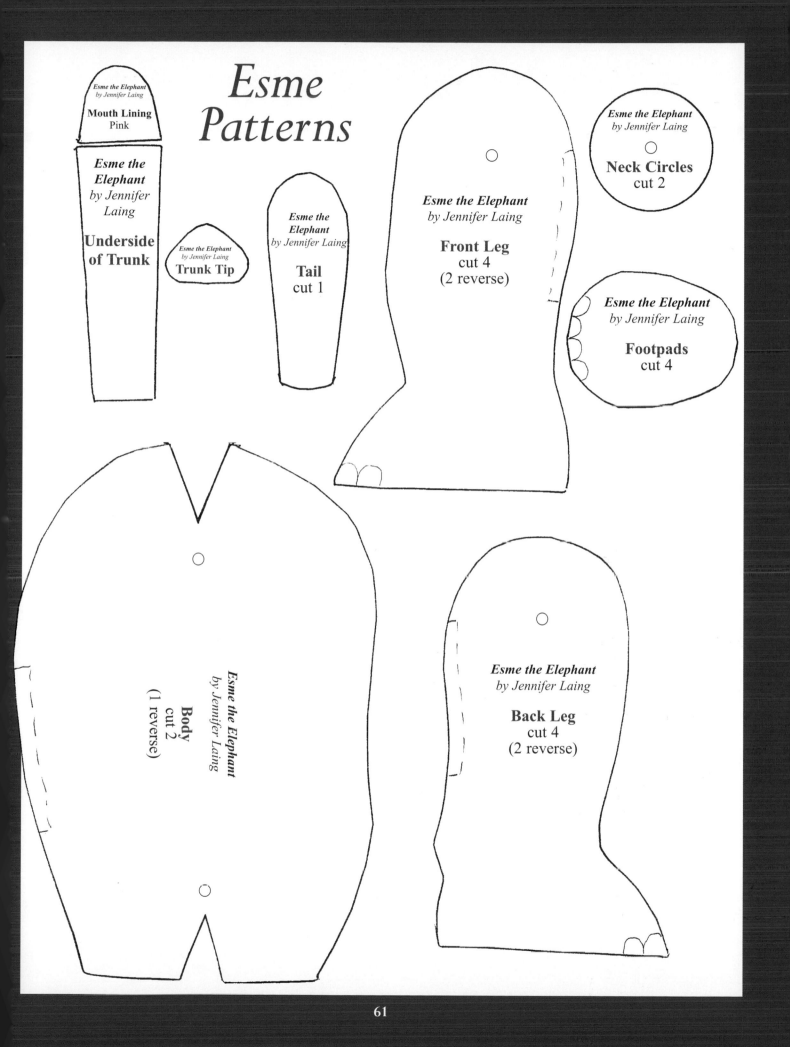

Esme the Elephant
by Jennifer Laing
Mouth Lining
Pink

Esme the Elephant
by Jennifer Laing
Underside of Trunk

Esme the Elephant
by Jennifer Laing
Trunk Tip

Esme the Elephant
by Jennifer Laing
Tail
cut 1

Esme the Elephant
by Jennifer Laing
Front Leg
cut 4
(2 reverse)

Esme the Elephant
by Jennifer Laing
Neck Circles
cut 2

Esme the Elephant
by Jennifer Laing
Footpads
cut 4

Esme the Elephant
by Jennifer Laing
Body
cut 2
(1 reverse)

Esme the Elephant
by Jennifer Laing
Back Leg
cut 4
(2 reverse)

On safari with Esme the Elephant (in upholstery velvet) and Baby Esme (in wool felt).

Viola
the Vervet Monkey

"Aping" around with Claudia the Chimp (in alpaca) and Viola the Vervet Monkey (in mohair).

Viola the Vervet Monkey and Claudia the Chimp
7in (18cm)

This is one pattern that can make either a chimp (or gorilla!) or a monkey. Chimpanzees tend to have flesh-colored faces, hands and feet, with dark hair. Their ears can be made to look more realistic by stitching two layers of Ultrasuede, and shading inside the curve of the ear. You can of course just use a single layer of Ultrasuede for a quick ear if you prefer. Monkeys often have darker color faces, hands and feet than their fur, and of course have tails.

Sewing the Head

The head looks more complicated than it is. The face, made out of Ultrasuede, is only one piece, and is sewn first. As in Fig. 27, sew the darts closed down the middle of the forehead and on either cheek. Then sew together the wider darts which will form the sides of the jaw, created by pinning A to A and B to B as also shown in Fig. 27. The face is now ready to be sewn into the head.

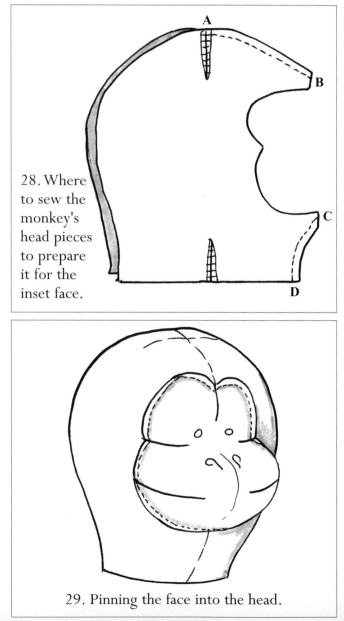

28. Where to sew the monkey's head pieces to prepare it for the inset face.

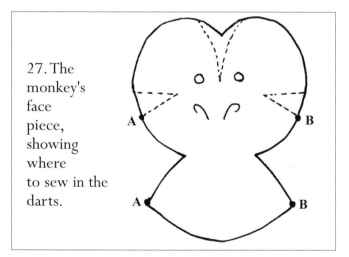

27. The monkey's face piece, showing where to sew in the darts.

The head needs to be partially sewn before inserting the face piece. First sew closed the darts at the top of the head and at the neck. Next, sew the two side head pieces together from A to B and from C to D, as in Fig. 28. Leave the back of the head open for ease of sewing in the face. Pin in the face, as in Fig. 29 and sew it in place. The back seam of the head can now be sewn closed, and the head turned through.

29. Pinning the face into the head.

Sculpting the Head

After the head is stuffed, it will need to be needle-sculpted in order to give it the desired features. Make sure your stuffing is not too hard, but rather even and pliable. Take a strong thread in a color that matches the face, and use a needle that is long enough to pass through the head. Start with a big knot and come through the head from the open neck. Bring your needle out at the center of the eye seam line A1 on Fig. 30. Tug your thread to make sure it is secure before starting. To form an eye socket, make a stitch across A1 to the edge of the eye dart, bringing it out centrally again at A2 on the mouth seam line. To form half the mouth, stitch across A2, and pull up tightly to B1, which is right next to where you started from at A1. Repeat on this side, stitching across B1 to the edge of the eye dart, then down to B2 centrally and stitch across to the edge of the mouth seam line. Pull back up to B1 where you started this side from, then across to C and from there stitch through to D and pull again. Knot off back at the neck opening.

This should give you the shape you need, but you can always add more stitching to create brow ridges, dimples, nostrils etc, if you are feeling adventurous. Otherwise you can simply draw on the nostrils, and then sew in the eyes, as marked in Fig. 29.

Sewing the Feet

The feet pieces are placed in pairs, with the thumb-like big toes facing inward. Make a small slit on the top of each foot, to be able to turn the piece through, as in Fig. 31. Sew each foot all the way around, and turn it through the slit. Stuff it softly, and ladder-stitch the slit closed. Continue with the same thread, and stitch toes into the foot, as shown in Fig. 32. Knot off in the slit area. The ankle area of the leg will cover this slit.

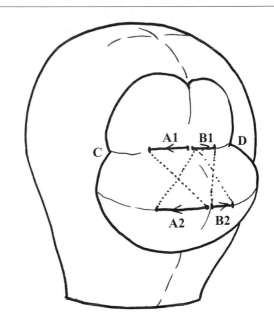

30. Needle-sculpting the eyes and mouth.

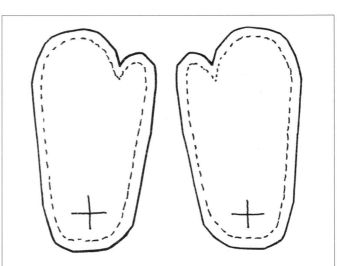

31. How to sew and turn the pair of feet.

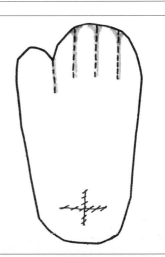

32. The stitching through the stuffed feet to create toes.

Sewing the Legs

Sew each leg up as normal, and turn through the opening, leaving the ankle area open. Place your joint in the top of the leg, and stuff, from both the joint opening and the opening at the ankle. Ladder-stitch the joint opening closed, and pin the open ankle on top of the prepared foot, covering the slit on the foot. Make sure that you have the correct foot on the correct leg. The big toes should be on the inside of the leg, that is, the same side of the limb as the shaft of the joint sticking out of the inside of the thigh, as in Fig. 33. Ladder-stitch the leg onto the foot all the way around the ankle and knot off. The closed and finished leg can now be jointed to the body. If you are using locknuts and bolts for jointing, you will have to joint the leg onto the body before closing the joint's open seam. In this case just stuff the leg to the knee, sew on the foot, joint the limb to the body, and then finish stuffing the top of the leg and close it.

Sewing the Arms

Each of your four arm pieces will have a matching hand, so place them in pairs before you start, making sure the thumbs are facing up on each hand. Attach each hand to each arm, then sew together your arms as normal, leaving the joint opening to turn the pieces through. When turned through, place in the joint and softly stuff the hand to the wrist. Using your 3in (8cm) doll needle and strong thread in a matching color to the hand, bring your needle through the opening and out at the center tip of the hand. Stitch to create fingers, as in Fig. 34. Knot off and pull the thread inside the arm. Finish stuffing the arm, ladder-stitch closed and attach the finished arm to the body. (You will need to attach the arm first before stuffing and closing if you are using locknuts and bolts instead of cotter pins.)

The Tail

If you are making a monkey you can give it a tail, using the pattern. It can either be sewn and turned through, or sewn with ladder-stitch from the outside if you have trouble turning long thin pieces through. A pipe cleaner placed down the length of the tail works well, and if it is a fat pipe cleaner you will not need to use additional stuffing. Have a short length (about ½in [1cm]) of pipe cleaner

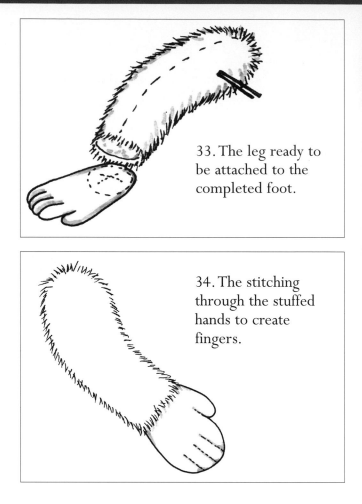

33. The leg ready to be attached to the completed foot.

34. The stitching through the stuffed hands to create fingers.

protruding from the base of the tail. When the body is finished and stuffed, make a hole with an awl where you want the tail to sit, and push in the extra length of pipe cleaner to secure the tail. Ladder-stitch the tail onto the body, all around the base of the tail, tucking the raw edges under as you go.

Material Required

Mohair- 11¾in x 11¾in (30cm x 30cm) square with a ⅜in (.9cm) pile.
Ultrasuede- 6in x 8in (15cm x 20cm) piece.
Eyes- pair of 4mm glass
Joints- 10 - 1in/25mm discs.
  5 - mini T-shaped cotter pins, or locknuts and bolts.
Pipe cleaner for the tail, if required.
Polyfill stuffing.

Viola and Chimp Patterns

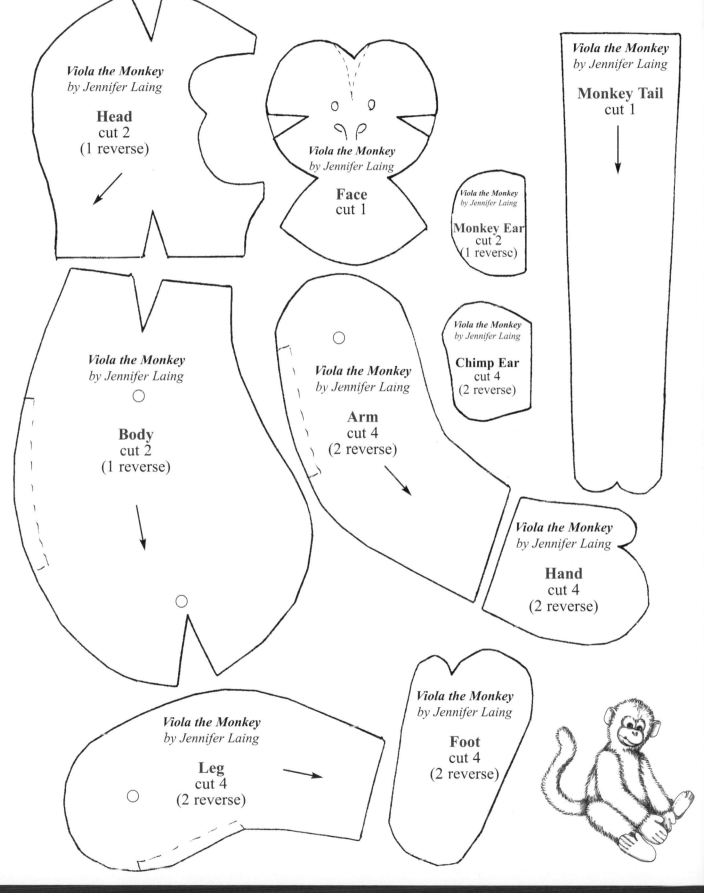

Viola the Monkey
by Jennifer Laing

Head
cut 2
(1 reverse)

Viola the Monkey
by Jennifer Laing

Face
cut 1

Viola the Monkey
by Jennifer Laing

Monkey Ear
cut 2
(1 reverse)

Viola the Monkey
by Jennifer Laing

Monkey Tail
cut 1

Viola the Monkey
by Jennifer Laing

Body
cut 2
(1 reverse)

Viola the Monkey
by Jennifer Laing

Arm
cut 4
(2 reverse)

Viola the Monkey
by Jennifer Laing

Chimp Ear
cut 4
(2 reverse)

Viola the Monkey
by Jennifer Laing

Hand
cut 4
(2 reverse)

Viola the Monkey
by Jennifer Laing

Leg
cut 4
(2 reverse)

Viola the Monkey
by Jennifer Laing

Foot
cut 4
(2 reverse)

Asia

As Asia was my birthplace and home for my formative years, I still have a strong connection with it. There are many amazing animals in different Asian countries, but it is the Chinese panda that captures most people's imagination. This charming animal is now a highly endangered species, and one that we may lose if it is not properly protected.

The panda is not a bear, and so has quite a different shape to either a realistic bear or an old-fashioned teddy bear. A panda's shape is plump and squat, with rather short limbs and a slumping posture. He has a big head with a high forehead, and a short muzzle with a shallow, wide nose. His face and patches over his eyes give him an endearing, youthful appearance, and one which is rather similar in shape to another youthful bear, Winnie-the-Pooh.

Phoebe the Panda

Phoebe
An 8in (20cm) Panda

The panda can be made in black and white, but looks just as good in brown and ivory as a 'dirty panda', or even in other color combinations. The fur looks fantastic when it is dense and not too long, so dense mohair, alpaca or even quality woven-backed synthetics work for this pattern.

The pattern has inset eye patches, an inset chest and the eyes are backed with brown Ultrasuede. The feet have detailed toes, but they are not as fiddly to do as they might appear!

The Head, Eye Patches and Felt-Backed Eyes

The head has darts to give it a little extra 'panda' shape, and it has a cut-out for the black eye patch. Sew the darts closed first, then pin and sew in the black eye patch, making sure the fur direction of the black patch matches that of the head for a realistic effect. This is a fiddly little piece, but it works, and it looks better than appliquéing the patch on over the top of a stuffed head. After the patches are sewn-in, the head is sewn together as normal (that is, the sides of the head are sewn from the tip of the nose down to the neck, then the gusset is sewn-in with the muzzle area sewn first to center it.)

Once the head is completed, it can be turned through and stuffed. Needle-sculpt the eye sockets, and pull up the corners of the mouth (See the Elf face Fig. 12 for details). The eyes can then be sewn-in, but first cut small circles in brown Ultrasuede just slightly larger than the eyes themselves. When your eyes are threaded up on your doll needle and ready to insert into the head, thread one of these circles behind each eye. As you pull the eye into the head, the circle of Ultrasuede will line the back of the eye and show around the rim of the eye.

Adjust if necessary as you pull in the eyes before you knot them off. Now the black eyes will be more visible against the black of the eye patches!

The Nose

The panda has been given a waxed template nose like the four-legged bear Ickabod. That is, the stitched nose is sewn over a leather or Ultrasuede base shape and pulled tightly to give it a rounded, slightly bulbous shape. The finished nose is then waxed to give it extra shine. If you like this look, follow the instructions given for Ickabod's nose.

Alternatively, you could give him a shiny black leather nose by cutting the shape you desire, padding it a little with some stuffing (add it as you sew) and stitch it in place using a fine leather needle. Look at photos of real pandas to see that they have wide, shallow nose shapes, quite different to that of a grizzly bear or polar bear.

Inset Shoulder Strip

The body has black shoulders, just like a real panda, so the body has been cut across to allow this change of color. Sew this seam connecting black to white first on each body half, before sewing the body together around the outer edge, leaving the opening in his back and a small space centrally at the neck for the head joint. Try and ensure that you use white thread on the white areas and black thread on the black sections, or it may show when you stuff the body and put strain on the seams.

The Arms

Remember what was said in the Introduction about the arms and the pawpads in this pattern. Refer back to it if necessary when you pin the inner and outer arm pieces together.

Appliquéd Toes

Cut the base pad shapes out of black Ultrasuede, and the toe details out of brown Ultrasuede. Pin and sew them on, allowing the seam allowance all around the edge to remain clear, as in Fig. 35A. Just before closing each section, stuff it to pad it out. Do this with each black pad before sewing them into the limb ends. Turn the legs through, joint them and stuff the feet and paws up to the ankle. Using a single strong black thread (such as an upholstery thread like Mastex), stitch across each padded toe strip, using three stitches equally spaced to divide the strip into four toes. Pull firmly between each stitch and maintain the tension to create the toes, as in Fig 35B. Knot off at the edge of the footpad in the mohair.

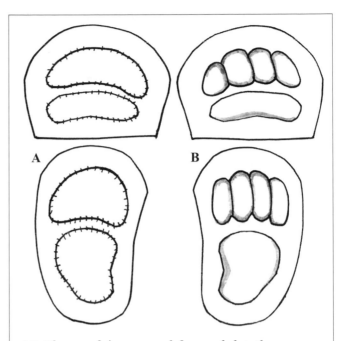

35. The panda's paw and footpad details, sewn on with ladder-stitch and stuffed, then the toe section divided with stitches.

Materials Required

Mohair or alpaca in a ½in (1cm) pile
   black, 12in x 9in (31cm x 23cm)
   white, 10in x 8in (25cm x 20cm)
Ultrasuede- black, 4in x 4in (10cm x 10cm)
   brown, 3in x 3in (8cm x 5cm)
Eyes - 6mm black glass or boot buttons
Joints -6 -1¼in (30mm) discs for the legs and head.
4 - 1in (25mm) discs for the arms.
5 - cotter pins or nuts, bolts and washers.
Black DMC#5 for nose and mouth.
Polyfill stuffing.

Phoebe the Panda made of alpaca and mohair, with a waxed template nose and appliqué pawpads.

Phoebe Patterns

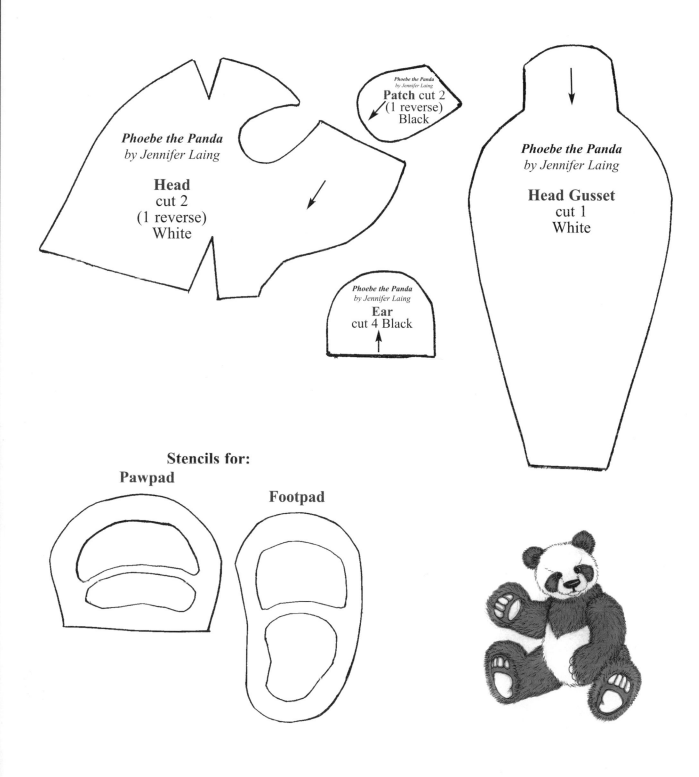

Phoebe the Panda
by Jennifer Laing

Head
cut 2
(1 reverse)
White

Phoebe the Panda
by Jennifer Laing
Patch cut 2
(1 reverse)
Black

Phoebe the Panda
by Jennifer Laing

Head Gusset
cut 1
White

Phoebe the Panda
by Jennifer Laing
Ear
cut 4 Black

Stencils for:

Pawpad

Footpad

Phoebe Patterns

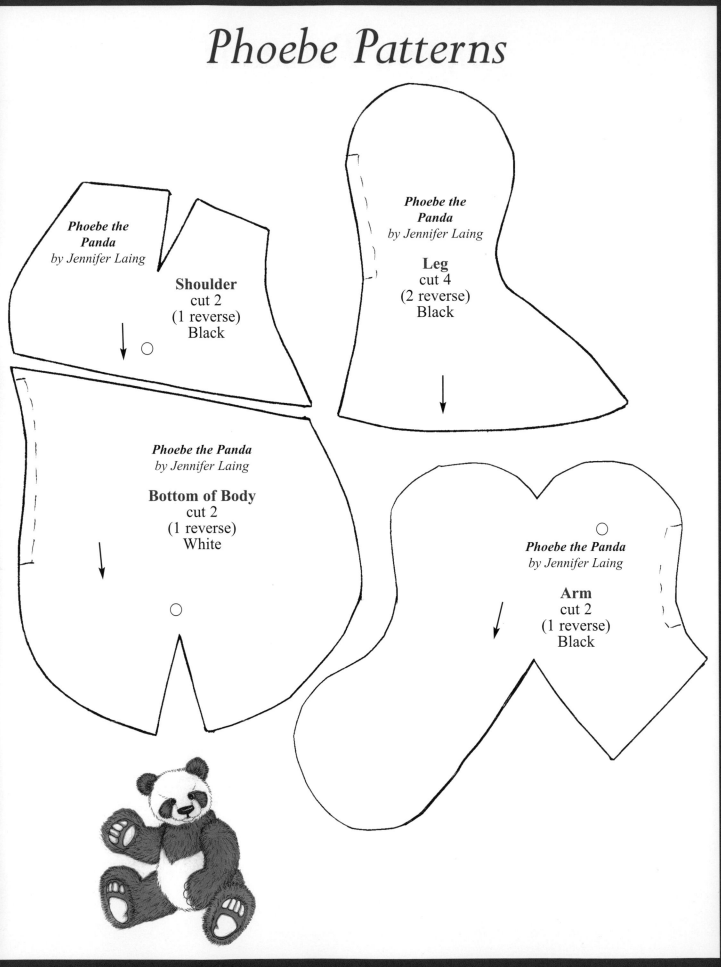

Phoebe the Panda
by Jennifer Laing

Shoulder
cut 2
(1 reverse)
Black

Phoebe the Panda
by Jennifer Laing

Leg
cut 4
(2 reverse)
Black

Phoebe the Panda
by Jennifer Laing

Bottom of Body
cut 2
(1 reverse)
White

Phoebe the Panda
by Jennifer Laing

Arm
cut 2
(1 reverse)
Black

Australia

Australia's fauna is unique, and is a huge, fascinating land. As well as including a couple of the country's famous animals, the koala and the emu, it seems only fair that one of Australia's infamous animals should make an appearance as well. Rabbits were introduced to Australia by the early settlers to provide a ready food source, but they quickly overran the country and became a pest. Now they are probably the most common animal in Australia, but they are certainly not the most popular with farmers!

Bluegum the Koala

Bluegum the Koala, enjoying her favorite snack.

Bluegum
An 8in (20cm) Koala (when sitting)

Although the koala is not one of the national animals of Australia, (the country's 'emblem' animals are the kangaroo and the emu) it is undoubtedly the best loved. Like all of Australia's mammals, they are marsupials or pouch-bearing animals, and their numbers have been greatly reduced by disease and loss of habitat.

Koalas are grey with brown eyes and a large black nose on a short muzzle, and they frequently have a white chin and white chest. They have tubby little bodies and large heads in relation to their bodies. As tree-dwellers, they have good claws, and also have two thumbs.

The pattern incorporates these observations by using a separate white chin gusset in the head, and stitching on the pawpad to suggest two thumbs. The nose is made out of padded leather, and as in the real koala, the ears are white on the inside and grey on the outside. Similarly, the chest has been inset to give his grey body a white chest. His body is stout and the slouched way that a koala sits is emphasised by the positioning of the legs.

Normally the joint is positioned centrally in the top of the limb, and is large enough to just about fill the space available. In order to create this relaxed pose, however, a deliberately undersized joint disc has been used, and placed in the rear of the limb. This has the effect of opening the leg, and this idea can also be used in other animals where this pose is desired.

The Head

The head is almost the same as that of a standard teddy bear, except there is an addition of a white strip between the two side head pieces, from the tip of the nose down to the neck edge. Sew in this piece first, to either side piece, as in Fig. 36. The gusset is then pinned and sewn-in as normal.

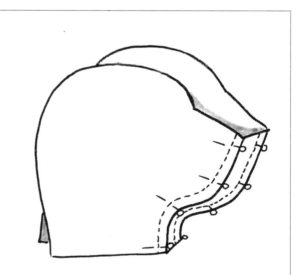

36. The koala's head, pinning in the white chin strip between the side head pieces.

The head is turned and stuffed, allowing a little springiness for needle sculpture, particularly between the eyes. Needle-sculpt between the eyes, and also pull up the corners of the mouth, as in the elf face Fig. 12.

Trim the mohair down in the nose area, equally over the upper grey area and the lower white area. The nose will sit about halfway over the top T-shape of the gusset seam.

The Nose

Cut the nose shape out of soft black leather and trim to fit the width of the muzzle. Make sure the leather is not too thick to sew, using a small, sharp leather needle. Slit the nostril lines, and glue the angles, as illustrated in Fig. 37A. Then slide them under the central septum strip until the edges touch underneath, as in Fig. 37B. This will give the nose a curved shape in profile.

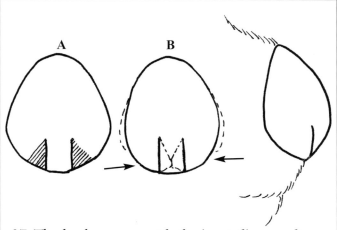

37. The leather nose, with the 'nostril' areas slit, glued and pushed underneath, creating a curved nose shape.

Before gluing the shaped nose in place, cut a smaller version of the leather nose without nostril slits and glue that in place. By allowing a ⅛in (.31cm) overlap with the nose over the base layer, it will be easier to sew, and create a rounded, padded shape. Pin and sew the leather nose on, using a single, fine black thread that is strong (Such as beading thread). If desired, you can stuff the nose before closing to add more padding.

The Inset Chest

As koalas usually have white chests, our koala has one too. As with any inset piece in a pattern, sew these pieces together first, then sew up the body halves together and finally sew all around the body edge, leaving the opening and a small space centrally at the neck for the head.

Paws and Claws

As with the small teddy bear and the panda, this koala pattern does not have a seam allowance for the wrist. This means that you will have to pin the inner and outer arms together carefully after you have sewn-in the pawpad. Follow the instructions in the Introduction to get the best results.

You can add whatever details you like to the koala's paw and footpads, but it is nice to define the double thumbs which is one of the koala's unique characteristics. This can be done by stitching through the stuffed paw, as shown in the pattern piece. Claws can also be stitched on, using a single black DMC #5 thread, and each stitch is brought over the feet and paws into the pad area to make them more visible.

Materials Required

Mohair- ½in (1cm) pile in dense grey,
   20in x 12in (51cm x 31cm)
white for chest, chin gusset and inner ears
   6in x 6in (15cm x 15cm)
Ultrasuede - grey to match the fur, 6in x 4in
   (15cm x 10cm)
Eyes - 8mm brown or black.
Joints - 2- 1½in/35mm discs for the head.
          8- 1¼in/30mm discs for the limbs.
          5- cotter pins or nuts, bolts and
             washers.
Black leather for the nose.
DMC# 5 for the mouth.
Polyfill stuffing.

Below: A Koala tea party, made from mohair, synthetics and wool by: (clockwise from top left) Marlene De Lorenzo, Julie Blake, the author, Wendy Cosford and Lesley Neuhaus.

Bluegum Patterns

Bluegum the Koala
by Jennifer Laing

Head
cut 2
(1 reverse)

Bluegum the Koala
by Jennifer Laing

Ear
cut 2 Grey
cut 2 White

*Bluegum
the Koala*
by Jennifer Laing

**Leather Nose
Template**

*Bluegum the
Koala*
by Jennifer
Laing

Chin Strip
cut 1
White

Bluegum the Koala
by Jennifer Laing

Leg
cut 4
(2 reverse)

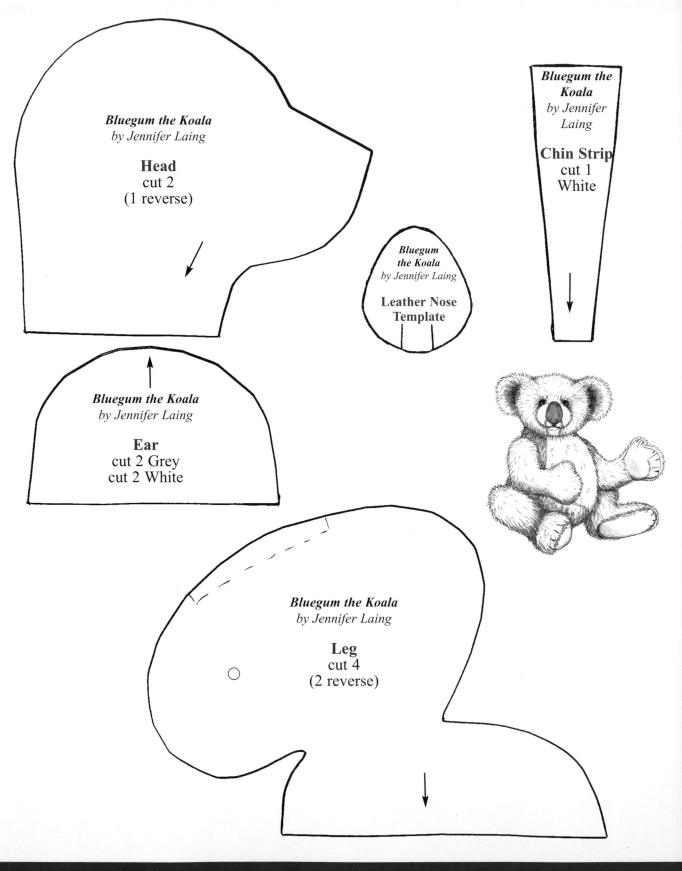

Bluegum Patterns

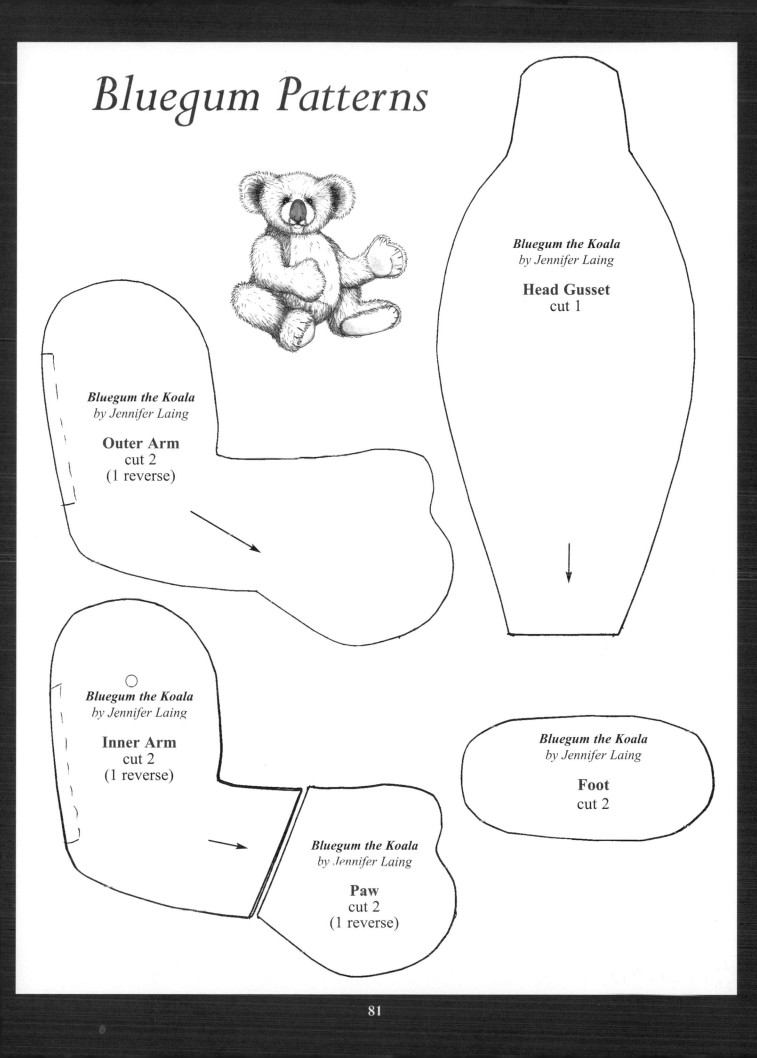

Bluegum the Koala
by Jennifer Laing

Head Gusset
cut 1

Bluegum the Koala
by Jennifer Laing

Outer Arm
cut 2
(1 reverse)

Bluegum the Koala
by Jennifer Laing

Inner Arm
cut 2
(1 reverse)

Bluegum the Koala
by Jennifer Laing

Foot
cut 2

Bluegum the Koala
by Jennifer Laing

Paw
cut 2
(1 reverse)

Bluegum Patterns

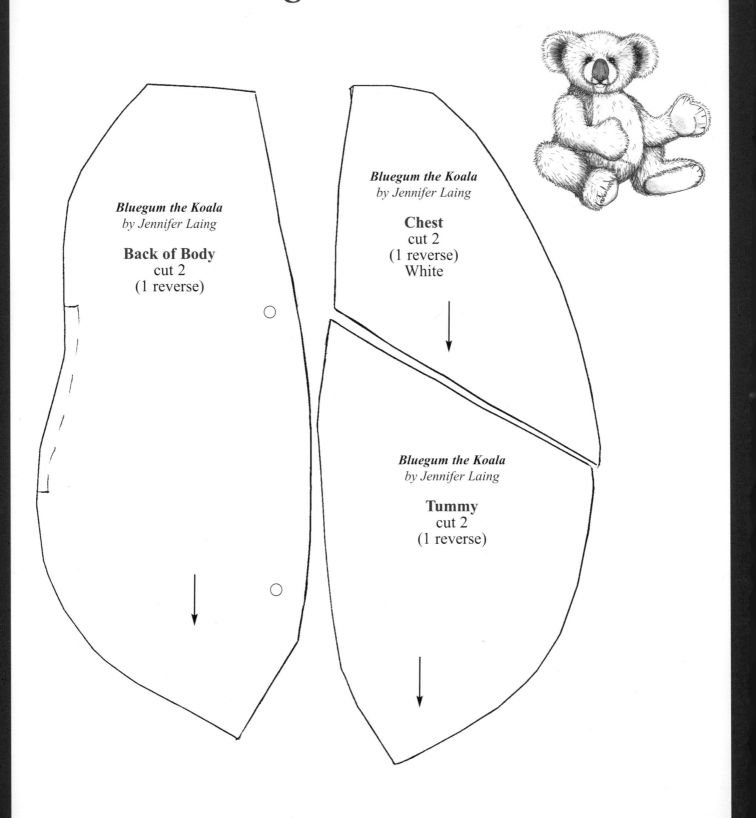

Bluegum the Koala
by Jennifer Laing

Back of Body
cut 2
(1 reverse)

Bluegum the Koala
by Jennifer Laing

Chest
cut 2
(1 reverse)
White

Bluegum the Koala
by Jennifer Laing

Tummy
cut 2
(1 reverse)

Ethel the Emu

Ethel the Emu, gone broody. (She hasn't noticed that her egg really is an ostrich egg, not an emu's!)

Ethel
A 12in (31cm) Emu (when standing)

Ethel the emu can be made in a variety of ways. You could give her strong legs to stand on, using pipe cleaners in the "drumsticks" of the legs, and fine glass beads in the feet for weight and stability. Alternatively you could softly stuff the legs with polyfill and glass beads for floppy legs, good for sitting around in the nest. Ethel could also be made in stripes and become a chick. Both emu and ostrich chicks have stripes and are a similar shape (although ostrich eggs are white, whereas emu eggs are dark green). If you make Ethel as an ostrich, remember that ostriches do have visible wings, while emus don't. While female ostriches are brown, the males are black with white tail and wing tips. Both male and female ostriches have almost featherless necks and heads, with long eyelashes, and the males have quite pink skin.

A few more natural history notes: -there used to be more than one species of emu in Australia, but early settlement caused three species to become extinct, and three more species are only known from fossil remains. They are the second-largest living bird, beaten only by the ostrich. (The emu stands five to six feet tall, while the ostrich stands eight feet tall.)

Long mohair works best for this pattern, as it simulates the soft feathers of these flightless birds. A great mohair for making up Ethel the emu is the long silver-tipped color often called Zotty. Ultrasuede in a soft brown or grey works well for the beak and legs. Glass eyes with painted details (there is a style known as the "buzzard" eye as it was originally made for taxidermy) are readily available and really suit a bird.

Needle-sculpture between the eyes helps define the eye sockets, and enables the eyes to sit closer together. Indelible marker pens in a grey or brown (depending on what color Ultrasuede is used) can shade the beak and legs, as well as mark out the nostrils and leg scales. Emus and ostriches have scale-like shapes down their legs and over the tops of their feet, just like chickens.

This pattern is quick to make, and a lot of fun. You could even give it a longer, curved beak and a shorter neck and turn the emu into a kiwi!

The Head

Ethel has a jointed neck and legs, and the neck has two circles of mohair, which cap each side of the joint rather than gathering the openings. See Fig. 38 for details. This is the same technique as used in Ickabod the four-legged bear pattern, in order to give the joint a smoother line and less bulging.

Sew the side head pieces together from the spot marked on the front of the head down to the front of the neck. Then pin in the gusset, and sew it in place. Turn the head through and stuff it, allowing a rim of fabric to sit above the stuffing in the neck. Pierce the center of one of the two mohair circles, place the neck disc on the fabric backing side and push a cotter pin through the disc and the mohair circle. Place this joint fur side out in the stuffed neck opening, and ladder-stitch shut around the neck. You now have a closed head with the joint protruding. Before attaching it to the body, add the beak, needle-sculpt the eye socket and sew in the eyes, as described below.

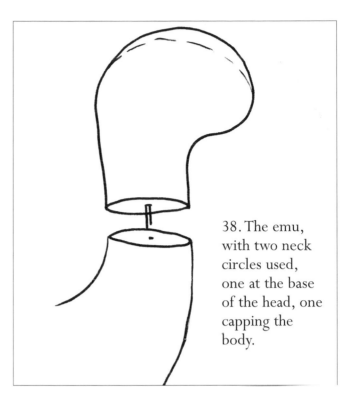

38. The emu, with two neck circles used, one at the base of the head, one capping the body.

The Face

Sew the two beak pieces together, turn through and stuff. Pin the beak in place on the front of the head, getting the angle of the beak right (it should be only slightly angled down) as in Fig. 39. Ladder-stitch in place, adding a little more stuffing before the final closing if necessary. Mark the nostrils and beak edge with your art markers.

Once the beak is in place you will be able to see where the eyes should go. Birds' eyes sit fairly close to the beak (see the colored plate, and in Fig. 39). Before sewing in the eyes, create sockets by stitching between the eyes and pulling, with a strong thread on a doll needle. This simple needle sculpture will create deeper sockets and give your bird a more realistic look.

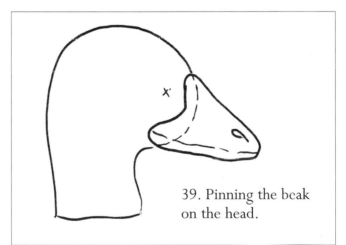

39. Pinning the beak on the head.

Thread up each eye on a strand of artificial sinew (split down if it is the thick type), put both ends of the thread through your doll needle and sew the eye into the head. Bring the threads from each eye out at the base of the neck, near each other, and knot together with a strong reef knot. Sink the knot and then cut the threads off short. The head is now finished and ready to be attached to the body.

The Body

The body is three pieces, with a tummy gusset giving extra shape and a flatter base to sit on. The body is left open at one side of the tummy seam, rather than on the top of the back. Jointing can be either cotter pins or nuts and bolts, but you might find it easier to use a cotter pin joint in the long narrow neck. This is because it is easier to reach with a fine cotter pin key than with a spanner or wrench.

Once the body is sewn, add the other small circle before turning it through. Sew this circle around the neck opening, capping the top of the body. The body can then be turned through and the head attached.

The Legs

The legs are made up in the same manner as the monkeys, with the feet being finished separately and then attached to the partially stuffed leg, as in Fig. 40. See the section on the monkey legs for details.

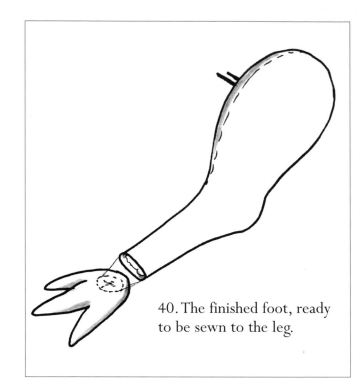

40. The finished foot, ready to be sewn to the leg.

Materials Required

Mohair- (in a tipped style works well) with a ¾in (2cm) pile or longer- 15in x 12in (38cm x 30cm)

Ultrasuede- (to match mohair, in a brown or grey)- 12in x 9in (30cm x 23cm)

Joints-2 - 1¼in (30mm) discs and cotter pins for legs.
       2 - ¾in (20mm) discs and cotter pin for neck.

Eyes- 8mm brown enamel painted glass ("buzzard" eyes work well for this bird).

Polyfill stuffing

Small glass beads/pellets.

Pipe cleaners for legs if the bird is to stand.

Indelible art marker pens for shading on beak and feet.

Ethel Patterns

Ethel the Emu
by Jennifer Laing

Underside of Beak
cut 1

Ethel the Emu
by Jennifer Laing

Top of Beak
cut 1

Ethel the Emu
by Jennifer Laing

Head
cut 2
(1 reversed)

Ethel the Emu
by Jennifer Laing

Body
cut 2
(1 reversed)

Neck

Ethel the Emu
by Jennifer Laing

Head Gusset
cut 1

Beak

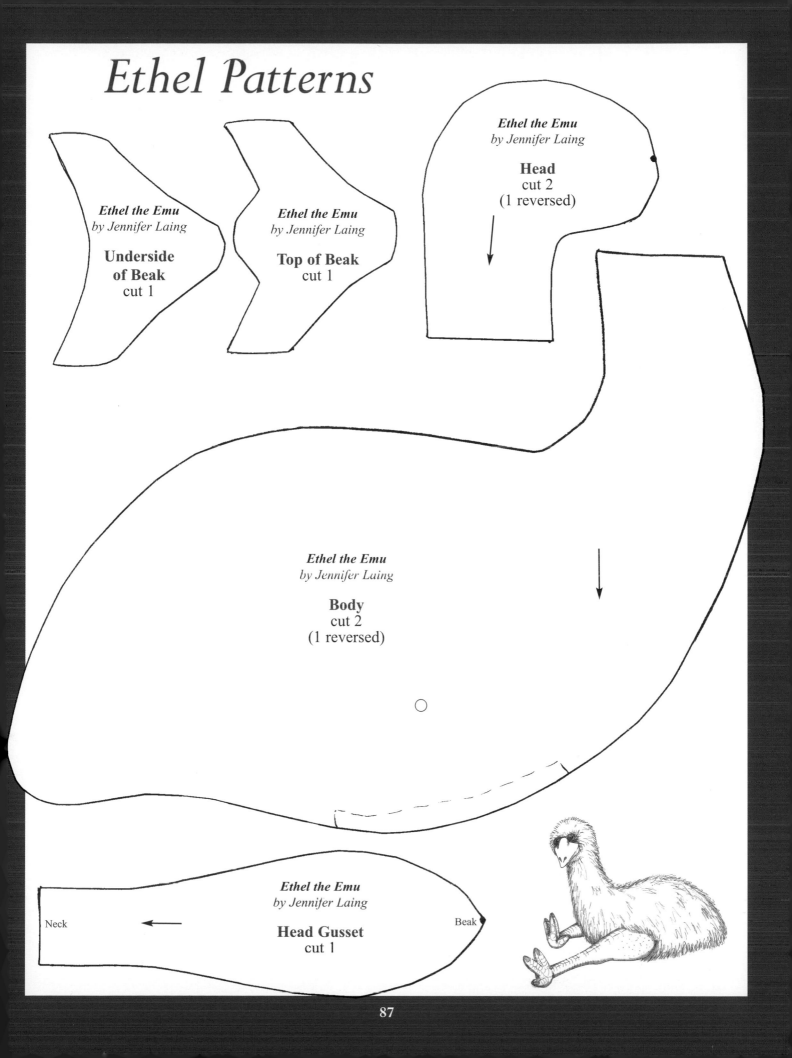

Neck

Ethel the Emu
by Jennifer Laing

Leg
cut 4
(2 reversed)

Ethel Patterns

Ethel the Emu
by Jennifer Laing

Tummy Gusset
cut 1

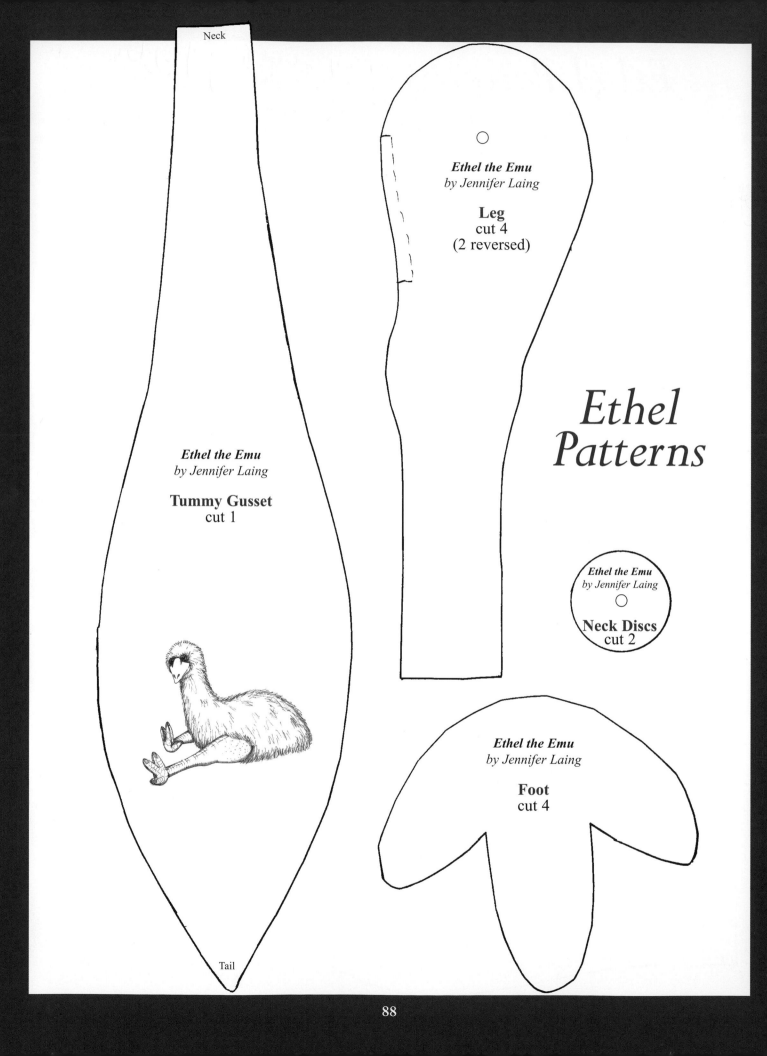

Ethel the Emu
by Jennifer Laing

○

Neck Discs
cut 2

Ethel the Emu
by Jennifer Laing

Foot
cut 4

Tail

Reggie the Rabbit

Reggie
A 9in (23cm) tall Rabbit (not including ears)

Although Reggie started off as a wild rabbit, we can also make him as a dwarf bunny with small ears, or a lop rabbit with long, floppy ears. He can also be made in some fun colors to become an Easter Bunny! Wild rabbits in Australia may have a bad reputation, but the domestic rabbit makes a good pet and has been bred in a wonderful range of colors, sizes and types. Have fun with this pattern and try it with the different ears!

This pattern has a simple two-piece body, "teddy baby" style arms, an inset nose lining and tufted whiskers. His tail is quite realistic, instead of the cotton ball-type tail found in many patterns. He can also have wired ears for extra pose-ability.

"Teddy Baby" Arms

This style of arm is so named because Steiff® first designed it for their Teddy Baby bear in the 1920s. This bear stood on large flat feet and looked like a funny bear cub, with his paws turned down rather than facing inwards as with a traditional teddy bear. These "teddy baby" arms are made in the same way as a leg, that is, the inner and outer limb are the same (except one has a joint spot) and the pad is sewn on after sewing the limb, like a footpad.

The pads on both the paws and feet can be detailed if you wish, either by painting, stitching or even appliqué.

Inset Nose Lining

This is a simple way of giving a very realistic look to your bunny's nose. First sew the two side head pieces from the spot marked on the nose down to the front of the neck. Then pin in the gusset, but only sew from the spots marked on the gusset back towards the edge of the neck, leaving a small diamond-shaped opening at the nose, as in Fig. 41.

Take your small diamond-shaped pink Ultrasuede nose lining piece, and pin it in place in the

opening, then sew it in. Turn the head through and stuff, taking care not to get any stuffing in the upper nose point. With your pink DMC #5 thread (Single thread is fine), stitch the tip of the nose point down into the septum stitch to anchor it, then stitch in a mouth, also in Fig. 41.

Wired Ears

If you are making the bunny with long, floppy ears, you will need to weight the tips or wire them in order to get them to hang properly. This is easy to do. When you have sewn the ears, turn them through. Bend a pipe cleaner or a length of florist's wire to fit the curve of the ear, allowing ½in (1cm) to extend from the ends of each side of the ear. Push it in place, and stitch it in, as in Fig. 42.

When the head is stuffed and you are ready to attach the ears, mark where you want them, make small holes with an awl, and push in the wires protruding from the edge of the ears. The ears are then ladder-stitched on, turning the raw edges to the inside as you go. The inserted wires will add stability to the base of the ears, and enable you to pose the ears however you wish.

Needle Sculpture

Simple stitching between the eyes and pulling will create indented eye sockets. You can then sew in the eyes, as detailed elsewhere in the book. The eyes are best put in before the head is attached to the body, as you can then hide the knot under the neck.

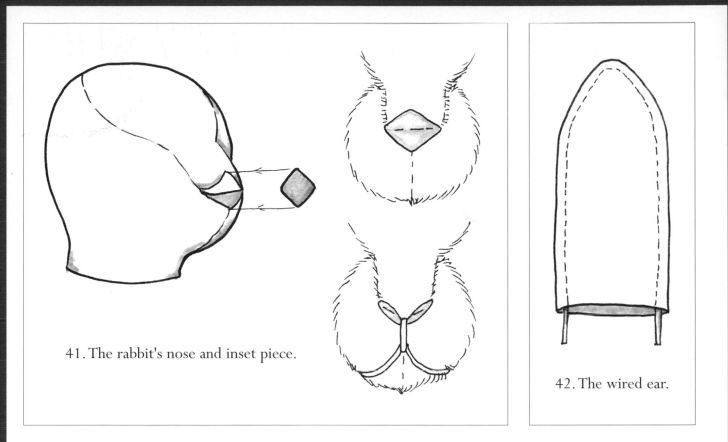

41. The rabbit's nose and inset piece.

42. The wired ear.

Tufted Whiskers

Whiskers really bring your bunny to life, and horsehair works wonderfully if you can find some. They are created in exactly the same way as Tom Collins the Pack Rat's whiskers, and see the description of tufting in the elf and gnome section.

The Legs

The legs are weighted with fine glass beads or pellets up to the ankle, then stuffed with polyfill around the joint. This will enable the rabbit to be balanced and he will stand unaided.

The Tail

This is a realistic tail and is sewn up of white on the outside, and the main body color for the side nearest the body. The tail is softly stuffed and sewn shut, and when the body is stuffed it is pinned in place, and ladder-stitched onto the body. Leave the tip free so that the tail angles slightly away from the body at the top just like a real rabbit's tail!

Materials Required

Mohair- ½in (1cm) pile or longer if making an angora bunny

20in x 12in (51cm x 30cm) scrap of white for the outside of the tail.

Ultrasuede in a flesh- tone 8in x 6in (20cm x 15cm)

Eyes- 8mm glass.

Joints- 6 - 1½in (35mm) discs for head and legs.

4 - 1in (25mm) discs for arms.

5 - cotter pins or nuts, bolts and washers.

Polyfill and pellets for stuffing.

DMC#5 in flesh for the mouth.

Horsehair for whiskers.

Reggie Rabbits, made in mohair and alpaca, and showing different ear types, by: (from left to right) Leanne Triggs, Susan Carroll, the author and Vicki-Lynn Smith. While the other rabbits have stitched noses, the author's has an inset nose, to show further variations on a theme.

Reggie Patterns

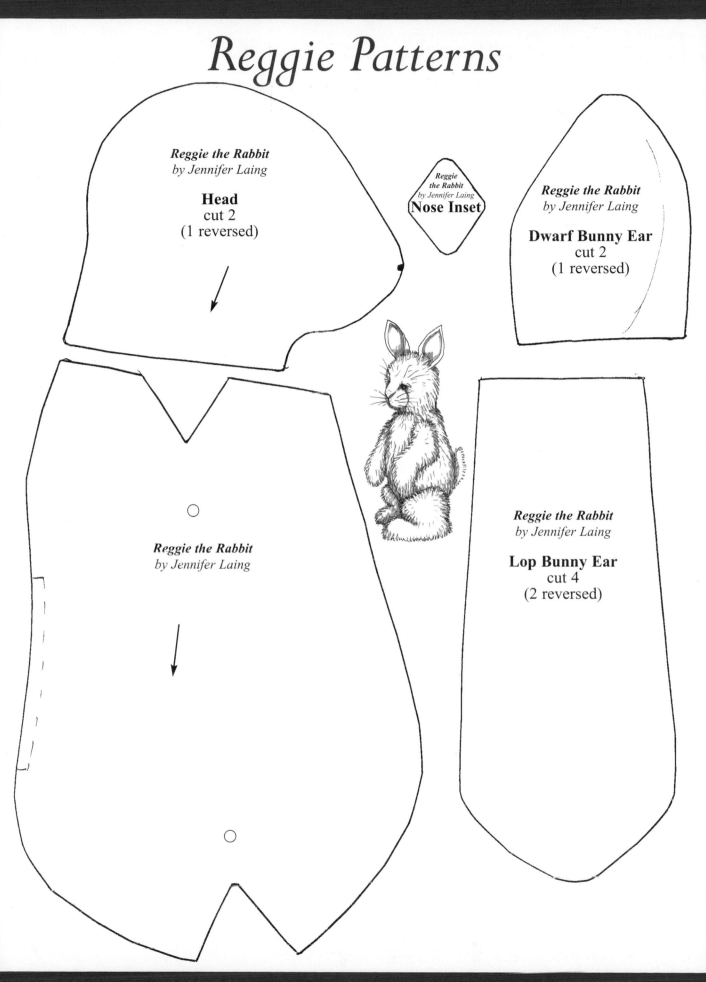

Reggie the Rabbit
by Jennifer Laing

Head
cut 2
(1 reversed)

Reggie
the Rabbit
by Jennifer Laing
Nose Inset

Reggie the Rabbit
by Jennifer Laing

Dwarf Bunny Ear
cut 2
(1 reversed)

Reggie the Rabbit
by Jennifer Laing

Reggie the Rabbit
by Jennifer Laing

Lop Bunny Ear
cut 4
(2 reversed)

Reggie Patterns

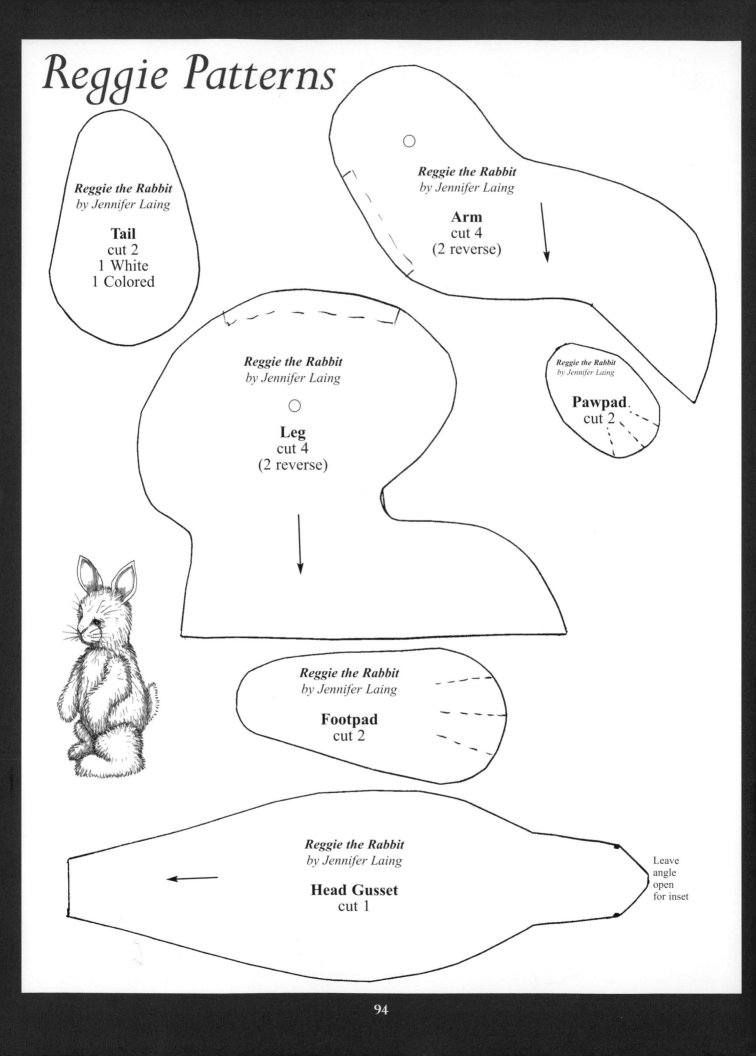

Reggie the Rabbit
by Jennifer Laing

Tail
cut 2
1 White
1 Colored

Reggie the Rabbit
by Jennifer Laing

Arm
cut 4
(2 reverse)

Reggie the Rabbit
by Jennifer Laing

Pawpad
cut 2

Reggie the Rabbit
by Jennifer Laing

Leg
cut 4
(2 reverse)

Reggie the Rabbit
by Jennifer Laing

Footpad
cut 2

Reggie the Rabbit
by Jennifer Laing

Head Gusset
cut 1

Leave
angle
open
for inset

Conclusion

I do hope you have enjoyed making up some of these little critters, and have learned some new techniques along the way. Creating something new can be a really freeing experience, as well getting you out of a rut in your life. It has been so cathartic for me to get away from just making bears, and to work on some different design problems for a while. It has also really put the fun back into bear making for me. It has been great to see the different responses people give when they see you make something as wacky as an emu or a rat. At the very least, it is worth it for the laughs! Life is too short to allow yourself to get bored, so try different things, it can lead you off in a whole new direction in life, and fill it with joy!

About the Author

Jennifer Laing is Australia's best known bear artist, and one of the first in that country, making her first bear in 1990. She was instrumental in getting the teddy bear business started in Australia, first through establishing a network for budding bear makers which she ran single-handedly for seven years (1991-98), then as sole organizer of the country's first all-bear shows. One of the favorite aspects of running a show for Jennifer is being involved in fund-raising for wildlife charities. She teaches all levels of bear making, right up to explaining the pattern and design process, and sharing her techniques in all areas

Mortimer and Phoebe, flanking the author's 4in (10cm) traveling companion Bertie.

of creating a bear or other animal. Her small workshops are extremely popular, and she teaches them in many countries. Jennifer enjoys writing books on the art of making bears, and sharing her love of all things furry. This is her fourth book, with more planned for the future. Her own bears have won international awards and are in high demand around the world.

Jennifer prefers to hand-stitch her bears, and consequently has a small output of rather small bears. Her favorite size range is four to eight inches, enough for a handful of love! While she doesn't have a large teddy bear collection, she does still have her precious childhood bears and animals, Bunrab, Poohbear, Tigger, Mopsy, Freddfox, Toto and friends. Jennifer says it is always comforting to be surrounded by your oldest and best friends.